PAINTING GREETING CARDS IN WATERCOLOR

PAINTING GREETING CARDS IN *Watercolor*

JACQUELINE PENNEY

Cincinnati, Ohio

I dedicate this book to all my wonderful students.

 Published by North Light Books, an imprint of F&W Publications, Inc., 1507 Dana Avenue, Cincinnati, Ohio 45207. (800) 289-0963. First edition.

Other fine North Light Books are available from your local bookstore, art supply store or direct from the publisher.

01 00 99 6 5 4

Library of Congress Cataloging-in-Publication Data

Penney, Jacqueline.
Painting greeting cards in watercolor / by Jacqueline Penney.—1st ed.
p. cm.
Includes index.
ISBN 0-89134-715-1 (pbk.: alk. paper)
1. Greeting cards. 2. Miniature painting—Technique. 3. Watercolor painting—Technique. I. Title.
ND2365.P46 1991
751.42′2—dc20 96-36396
CIP

Edited by Joyce Dolan
Production edited by Marilyn Daiker
Designed by Brian Roeth
Cover illustrations by Jacqueline Penney
Cover photography by Pamela Monfort Braun/Bronze Photography

About the Author

PHOTOGRAPH BY JANET T. SWANSON

If "Eyes are the mirror of the soul" then with the paintings of Jacqueline Penney, we enter the inner life explored by those eyes—the harmony of domestic still lifes, the tranquility of bucolic Long Island landscapes, the laughter captured in a line of laundry set dancing by the breeze.

Penney won a scholarship to the Phoenix School of Design. She also attended Black Mountain College in North Carolina, the Institute of Design in Chicago, and the Art Students League in New York. Her professional affiliations include the prestigious Salmagundi Club in New York City, National Association of Women Artists, National League of American Pen Women and the Miniature Art Society of Florida. Penney is listed in *Who's Who of American Artists*, *Who's Who of Women* and *Who's Who of Teachers*.

She has received several awards including the Award of Merit from the National League of American Pen Women, 1994; Best Landscape at the Mid-Atlantic Regional Watercolor Exhibition, 1990; the Erlanger-Seligson Memorial Award from the National Association of Women Artists, 1989. Teaching is her greatest source of gratification.

A native of Long Island, Penney continues to reside there in the small Cutchogue community where she has renovated an 1890s barn into a distinctive home and gallery. She is married to Jerry Moore who transforms their landscape into a floral inspiration of its own.

Acknowledgments

Many thanks to the editors at North Light Books: Greg Albert, Kathy Kipp, Joyce Dolan and Marilyn Daiker.

Table of Contents

My miniature watercolor greeting card and painting classes began because several students didn't understand how to plan a painting using a detailed thumbnail sketch. I offered a separate class for creating small black-and-white value sketches to be translated into very small watercolors. The exquisite miniature paintings that evolved from that class were not only useful, they were works of art.

JACQUELINE
PENNEY

PHOTOGRAPH BY MIKE RICHTER

You'll find that painting small saves time, space and money. Painting materials can be stored in a tote bag or box and easily assembled anywhere.

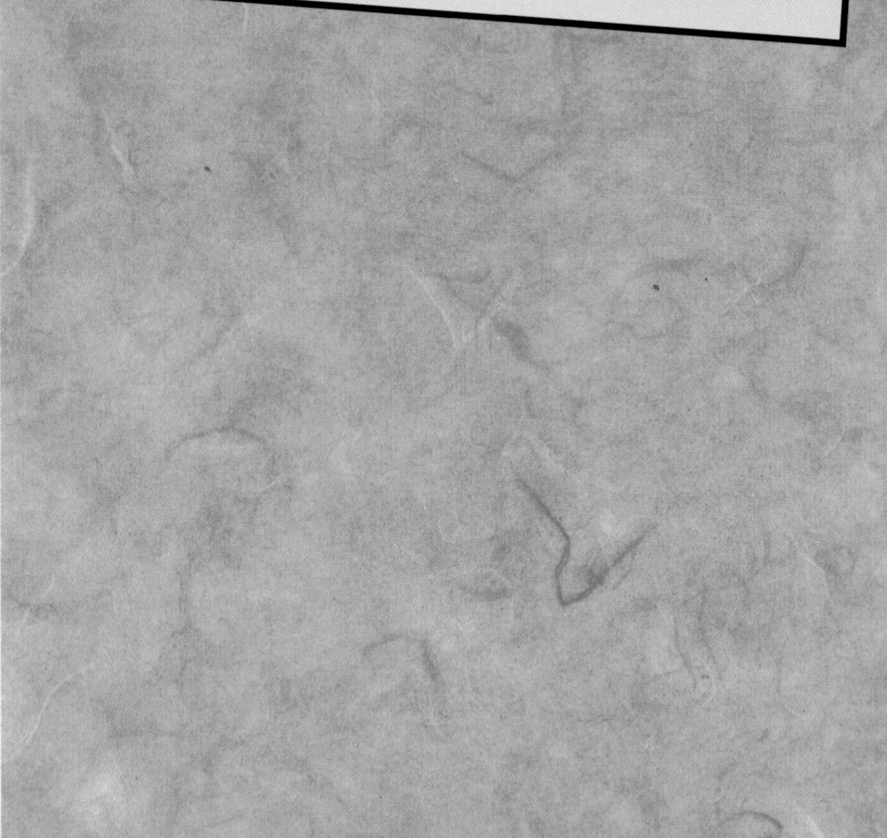

Chapter One

TOOLS, TIPS & TECHNIQUES

Learn what tools you'll need to start making beautiful watercolor greeting cards and gifts.

Tools

I encourage you to purchase a few very good brushes, tubes of professional paint and the best watercolor paper available rather than a lot of poor quality equipment. Painting small requires less materials but not less quality; good equipment, not a lot of equipment.

LIGHTING

Good lighting is important, especially at night. Invest in a balanced warm/cool lamp that extends over your work area. During the day, avoid painting in direct sunlight.

STORAGE

Watercolor materials can be made very compact, requiring very little storage space. If you are painting on location, it doesn't take long to set up on a park bench, at a picnic table or even in a waiting room. I keep my watercolor materials in my backpack, which fits under the seat in an airplane. It's also easy to carry, hangs on a hook, a quarter sheet of paper fits in it perfectly, and I can fit everything else I need into it with room to spare.

PAPER AND CARDS

Watercolor paper comes in different weights and textures. It can be purchased in spiral notebooks, blocks or rolls. The heavier the weight, the higher the price. I used Arches 140-lb. (300g/m^2) cold-press for all the demonstrations in this book and don't recommend using lighter weights.

I purchase full sheets of watercolor paper by the *quire*, which is a package of twenty-five sheets, because it's less expensive and I have plenty of storage space. If storage is a problem, however, buy one or two sheets at a time.

Folding the paper in half several times makes it rip apart very easily and leaves a nice deckled edge for the card. The halves can be torn into quarters for easy storage. I put the quarter sheets—which fit perfectly in my backpack—into a large Ziploc bag to keep them clean and dry. I also use postcard pads and ready-made blank cards with matching envelopes that are made for watercolors.

BACKING BOARD

I use a backing board made from lauan plywood, which is available at most lumber stores. Cut the plywood to 12½" × 16" (31.8cm × 40.6cm), then sand and varnish it several times to make it waterproof. Tape a quarter sheet of paper around the edges onto the backing board. Then measure the size of formats you want to use and separate each with 1" (2.5cm) of masking or drafting tape. (See the photo below.) Use the small space on the right side to test colors. You can also use the bottom area for that purpose and/or make it into gift tags.

The ½" (1.3cm) border around each painting, leaves ample room to mat or frame when the paintings are separated. A plastic clipboard, a waterproofed foamcore board, or even the lid of the John Pike palette can also be used for a backing.

A quarter sheet of paper measured and taped onto a backing board to create small formats.

BRUSHES

Basically, there are two kinds of watercolor brushes: flats and rounds. They all have short handles and come in sizes from no. 000, which is very small, to very large. Good quality synthetic brushes are less expensive than sable brushes. I test a brush in the art store by putting it into a glass of water: The tip of the round brush should come to a perfect point when the water is shaken out.

All the projects demonstrated in this book are painted with these brushes:

no. 2 and no. 6 rounds
no. 2 rigger or script
⅜-inch (10mm) or ¼-inch (6mm) flat

In a few demonstrations I use a larger brush to paint an area more quickly or drop in color for the wet-in-wet technique:

no. 10 round
1-inch (25mm) flat

PALETTES

There are many palettes to choose from. My favorite is a John Pike white plastic palette. It separates the paints in wells with a large mixing area in the center and has a lid to keep the paints moist or to use for extra mixing space. It also fits into my backpack. In a pinch I can use a white china plate for a palette. A butcher's tray is okay, but it's heavy.

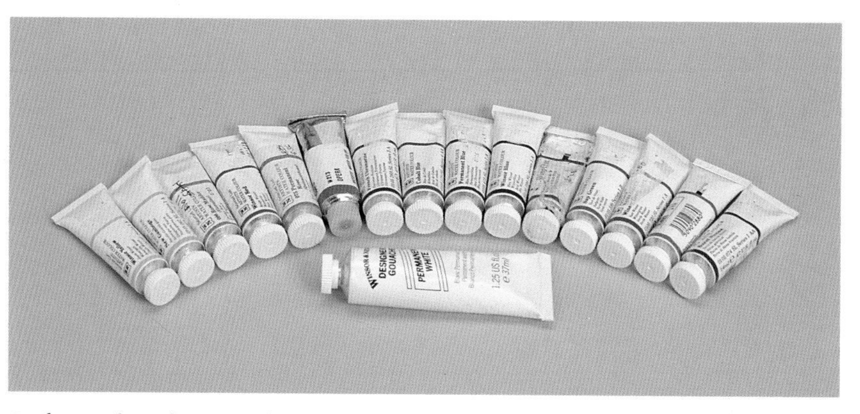

Professional-grade watercolors made by Winsor & Newton plus Opera by Holbein and one tube of gouache.

PHOTOGRAPH BY MIKE RICHTER

PAINT

There are many transparent watercolor paint manufacturers. I generally use Winsor & Newton professional transparent tube paint rather than the smaller student-grade tubes and intersperse other brands, such as Holbeins's Opera. I sometimes use Chinese White or acrylic white for spatter.

I occasionally use gouache, an opaque watercolor, to paint an object on top of watercolor such as in the Pure Fantasy project on page 112. Feel free to use transparent and opaque watercolor together. I suggest a limited palette of gouache colors: white, black, yellow, blue and red.

In the first three projects in this book, I begin simply with a limited palette of Aureolin Yellow, Rose Madder Genuine and Cobalt Blue. We'll continue to add new pigments as the projects progress.

Pike palette with separate color wells, a large mixing area and brushes.

PHOTOGRAPH BY MIKE RICHTER

COLOR PALETTE

Here is a list of the paints used for the projects in this book. Watch for the color wheel at the beginning of projects. Each time a new color is added to your palette, you'll see the color wheel.

Aureolin Yellow
Rose Madder Genuine
Cobalt Blue
Cerulean Blue
Ultramarine Blue
Winsor Yellow
Winsor Red
Winsor Blue
Winsor Green
Permanent Rose
New Gamboge
Burnt Sienna
Raw Sienna
Neutral Tint
Scarlet Lake
Opera
Mauve
Sap Green

A NOTE ON COLOR

If you really want a bare-bones palette, purchase a warm and a cool version of each primary color. All the rest can be mixed. It's more convenient to have all the colors laid out in front of you, but learning to mix color is what it's really all about.

MASKING FLUID

Use masking fluid to maintain the white of your paper. It resembles rubber cement, sticks to the paper, and when dry can be rubbed off. It will also stick to your brush unless the brush has a wet soapy solution on the bristles. Wash your brush thoroughly with warm water after using masking fluid.

Allow the masking fluid to dry before you paint over it. The paint must then dry before you remove the mask. Rub it off gently with clean fingers or use a commercial mask lift-off, which is less likely to smudge. There are many brands of masking fluid to choose from, but for the demonstrations in this book I used Winsor & Newton Masking Fluid, which has a tint of yellow.

WAXED PAPER

Another way to *resist* color is to lay a piece of waxed paper over the drawing and burnish your design onto the paper. The waxed area will remain permanently white, because once the wax is on the paper, it can't be removed.

Wax works better than masking fluid in some cases. For example, it's difficult to put masking fluid into a tiny space and maintain a sharp edge. Thin lines, calligraphy or small designs can be achieved by burnishing the wax onto the paper. Experiment to learn which technique works best for you.

TRACING AND TRANSFER PAPER

Use these tools to trace a photograph or drawing and transfer it to your watercolor paper. Transfer paper is easy to erase and comes in several colors.

TAPE

I prefer 1" (2.5cm) drafting or masking tape because it doesn't tear the paper when you remove it.

PENCIL AND PENS

A mechanical no. 2 pencil is good for drawing because the point stays sharp. For signing I use a no. 01 Pigman Micron pen, which comes in a variety of colors, or a Rotring Rapidograph with a .25mm point.

RULER AND ANGLE

A 12″ (30.5cm) ruler is all you'll need for the projects in this book. A small plastic angle is helpful to square a corner so that measurements are accurate.

WATER BOTTLE

A small spray-and-pour bottle made by ArtBin holds water in two compartments; one pours and the other sprays. This is great to use both on location and in the studio. I use two plastic containers to hold water—one for cleaning brushes and the other for mixing colors.

TISSUES, TOWELS AND SPONGES

These tools are a must for picking up drops and spills and for pulling water out of a brush. On location I take a half roll of toilet tissue in my backpack instead of towels because it doesn't take up as much room.

A natural sponge is useful to wet an area with clean water or to use with pigment to create texture. A damp flat sponge kept in your Pike palette will also keep the paints moist.

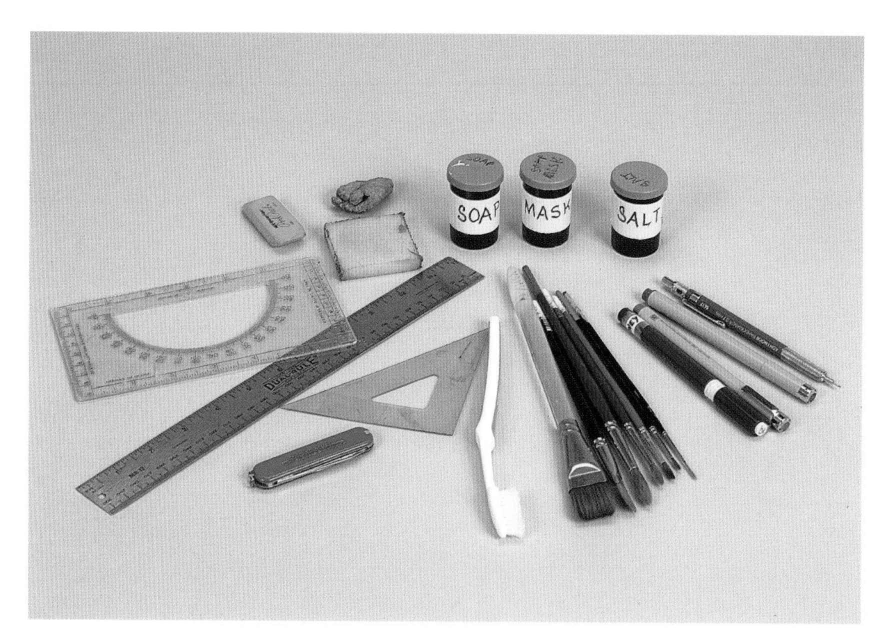

It's handy to carry soap, masking fluid and salt in labeled film canisters. The other equipment shown here are Pink Pearl and kneaded erasers, a small knife, a toothbrush used to spatter, several brushes, a mechanical pencil and pens, a mask remover that resembles an eraser, a ruler and an angle.

PHOTOGRAPH BY MIKE RICHTER

CAMERA, PHOTOGRAPHS AND INSPIRATION

I keep a compact Olympus 3500 and zoom lens with me most of the time. What do I do with these photographs? File them! I sort the photos into categories such as animals, birds, boats, people, rocks or barns and file them in a tabletop dual-file drawer so I can easily find a subject I'm looking for. When I need a little inspiration, there's always something in the file that ignites my imagination.

The bare minimum. When I want to travel light, I can do very well with a no. 2 round and a ⅜-inch (10mm) square tip or just the brush that comes with a Cotman Field Box. Postcards fit in my pocket, or I may take just my sketchbook. I carry enough drinking water to supplement the small container that comes with the Cotman Box.

Here's a variety of paper and palettes to choose from when going on location.

PHOTOGRAPH BY MIKE RICHTER

Basic Techniques

Here are examples of the basic techniques I use to paint the greeting cards and gifts in this book.

Flat wash: Color is applied evenly, usually on dry paper, with no gradation of value.

Wet-into-damp wash: Color is applied to damp paper, where it spreads but maintains soft edges.

Blending or charging: Color is charged into a wet color wash and allowed to mingle.

Graded wash: Color is applied from dark to light value.

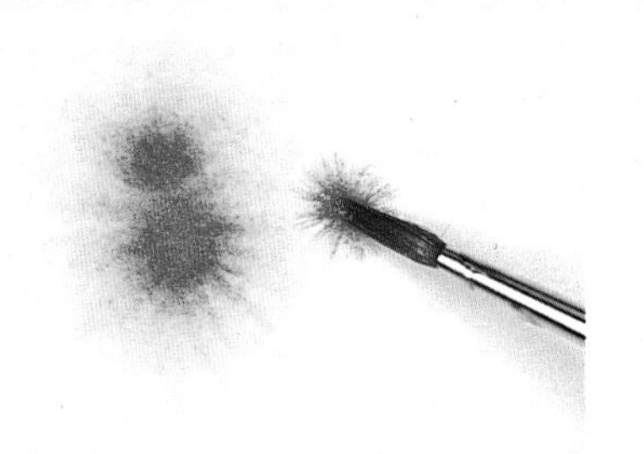

Wet-in-wet: Color is applied to or dropped on wet paper, allowing it to spread in an unpredictable way.

Glaze or layered wash: Color is applied on top of another color that is dry and modifies them both.

Lost and found edges: One edge is defined and the other washed away quickly before paint can set, leaving no definition.

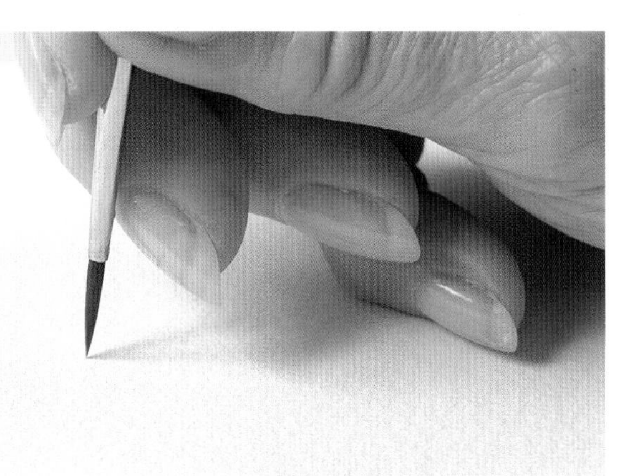

Dotting: The tip of a round brush is used to create tiny dots or dash strokes.

PHOTOGRAPH BY MIKE RICHTER

Side loading: Dipping one side of a clean, damp brush into pigment is called side loading. *When the brush is drawn across the paper, one edge is defined and the other is not.*

Lifting out: Wet or dry pigment is removed by stroking with a thirsty clean brush or scrubbed out with sponge, brush or toothbrush.

Resists: Applying wax crayon or burnishing waxed paper onto the watercolor paper will cause it to resist the pigment. However, the wax cannot be removed. Liquid masking fluid resembles glue and is painted onto the paper to resist pigment, but it can be removed when the paint is dry.

Some Notes on Color

I want to convey a few basic principles of color theory, and I'll keep it very simple. If you're interested in learning more about color, I highly recommend you read Tom Hill's *The Watercolorist's Complete Guide to Color*, published by North Light Books.

There are three primary colors: yellow, red and blue. We have to buy them because we can't make them.

The secondary colors are orange, violet and green. We can buy them too, but we can also mix secondary colors by combining two primaries. For instance, mix yellow and red to make orange; mix blue and yellow to make green; and mix blue and red to make violet.

Colorists may designate one particular red, yellow or blue to be a true color on the color wheel, but there are lots of different primaries to choose from: bright (or hot) reds and cool reds, bright yellows and cool yellows, bright blues and cool blues. If you divide the color wheel down the center, the warm colors will be on the left—the yellows, oranges and reds. We can associate these colors with the orange sun, red hot peppers, or the warm Indian yellows of fall. On the right are the cool colors that we may relate to the cool green grass, the cold sky of winter, and so on. Each color has a *temperature*. For example, New Gamboge Yellow is warmer than Winsor Yellow; Ultramarine Blue is warmer than Cerulean Blue. The subtle differences become apparent with practice.

Complementary colors are opposite one another on the color wheel. To gray down a green, for instance, add a little red to it. The red neutralizes the intensity of the green. This is true for all the other opposites on the color wheel. An easy way to remember them is to associate the complementary colors with something else. Red and green are complementary—think of Christmas or Hanukkah. Yellow and violet—think of Easter or spring colors. Blue and orange—think of the Mets or Halloween.

A NOTE ON COLOR

- **Hue: Specific name of a color, such as, a blue sky, a yellow banana.**
- **Value: A color's lightness or darkness. Yellow is considered a light value and purple a dark value.**
- **Intensity: A color's strength or weakness. Color applied directly from the tube is at its full intensity.**
- **Tint: By adding water, you lighten or tint a color. In opaque painting, white paint is added to lighten the color.**
- **Shade or graying down: A color made darker by adding black, Neutral Tint or the color's complement.**

A color wheel. Arrows mark the primary colors: yellow, red and blue. The colors used here are Aureolin Yellow, Rose Madder Genuine and Cobalt Blue. Warm colors are on the left; cool colors are on the right. Complementary colors are opposite each other and mixed in the center triangles.

Painting watercolor greeting cards is a great outlet for your creativity plus you gain a one-of-a-kind gift for a special occasion.

Chapter Two

KEEP IT SIMPLE

Convert one basic, imaginary landscape into a variety of simple paintings by making slight variations.

The first three projects in this chapter are variations on one imaginary landscape theme. Using variations on a theme is a quick way to do many different cards at the same time. You can create three different paintings by making very simple changes in line, color and placement. The painting in the fourth demonstration becomes a seascape when you change the grassy meadow into a body of water and add sailboats. The paintings in the fifth and sixth demonstrations are of a well-known mountain called the Dome at Yosemite National Park.

Each painting illustrates a technique to practice, such as lifting out, graded washes, hard and soft edges and masking. We learn watercolor techniques as a musician learns a new piece of music—with practice.

BRUSHES AND PAPER YOU'LL NEED

- **¼-inch (6mm) square tip brush**
- **no. 2 round, which comes to a very sharp point**
- **no. 000 rigger**
- **quarter sheet 140-lb. (300g/m²) Arches cold-press watercolor paper, 11″×15″ (27.9cm×38.1cm)**
- **backing board**

For the first three demonstrations you'll use a limited palette of Aureolin Yellow, Rose Madder Genuine and Cobalt Blue; that is considered a delicate palette.

Tape the watercolor paper to a backing board that is slightly larger than the paper. Mask several formats with 1″ (2.5cm) drafting tape. This leaves 1″ between paintings. When the paintings are separated, the ½″ (1.3cm) border around each leaves ample room to tape it into a mat, or to trim and paste it onto a card.

PROJECT ONE

Lifting Out

Begin with a basic imaginary landscape and learn to create a variety of paintings for cards and gifts just by making slight variations of this one scene.

Painting Size: 1¾″ × 2¾″ (4.5cm × 7cm)

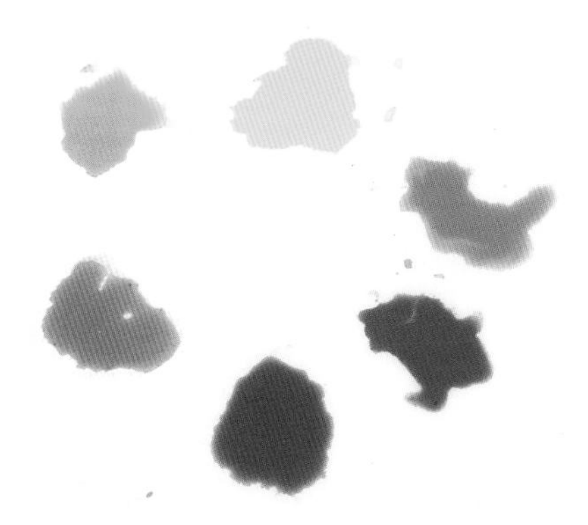

STEP ONE

Make ample puddles of Aureolin Yellow, Rose Madder Genuine and Cobalt Blue on your palette. Then mix secondary colors into puddles between the primaries to create a color wheel. Premixing saves time and prevents frustration.

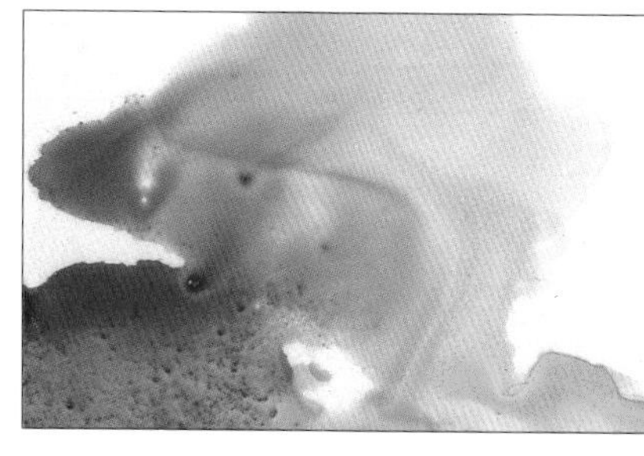

STEP TWO

Make an interesting light gray for the distant mountain range by mixing small combinations of purple, orange and blue. Keep the value very light by adding enough water to dilute the pigment. Test it on a piece of watercolor paper. Watercolor tends to dry lighter, so if you want to be sure about the color, dry the test swatch.

You will notice that the cool, light colors tend to recede and warm, dark colors tend to come forward. Each mountain range will become slightly darker and warmer as it approaches the viewer.

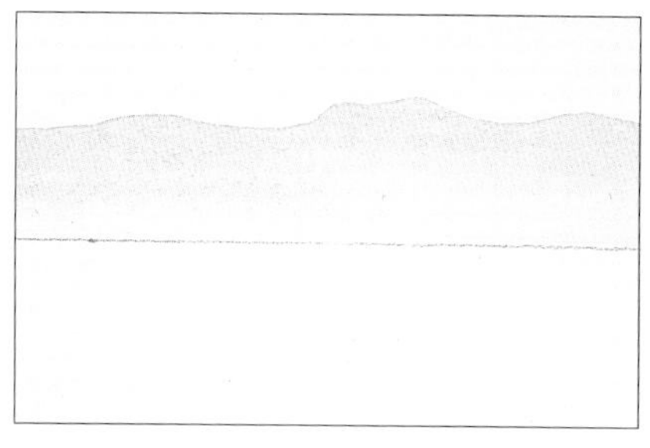

STEP THREE

With a no. 2 pencil, lightly draw a horizontal line 1″ (2.5cm) down from the top of the painting to indicate the horizon. Tilt the board slightly so the paint will run down. With a ¼-inch (6mm) square tip brush, paint the distant mountain range. Quickly clean the brush and touch the tip of it to a sponge or towel to draw out excess water, then draw the clean brush across the bottom of the previous stroke. This allows the pigment to bleed into the slightly wet area and disappear.

This is a very simplified graded wash. One edge is lost, the other is found; you've created a hard and a soft edge.

STEP FOUR

For a crisp, defined edge on the next mountain range, make sure the first area you painted is dry. If the paint is still wet, the new application will bleed into it. Mix a slightly darker variation of the gray by adding a little blue-violet to the original mixture. Test this next to the first color swatch used on the distant mountains to check that the new color is slightly darker and warmer. With a ¼-inch (6mm) square tip brush, paint in the next mountain range with irregular peaks and valleys. Lighten with a clean brush near the horizon line as in painting the first mountain range. Then let it dry.

STEP FIVE

Paint the nearest mountain range slightly darker and warmer all the way down to the horizon line without adding additional water. Clean the brush and dot in or charge in yellow with the tip of a round tip brush that is not too wet. The paper is already wet, and the pigment will mingle with the color underneath. Whenever a new color is added to an area still wet with pigment, the new color mingles and spreads into the first color. This process is called *charging*. The effect is to create fuzzy trees in the distance. The edges are not defined, and because the purple-gray is a near complement to yellow, it tones down the intensity of the yellow.

STEP SIX

Allow the paint to dry thoroughly and then paint the meadow a light yellow. A landscape is emerging, but there is no center of interest or a place for the eye to rest. Adding a small white steeple in the distance will help.

STEP SEVEN

Use drafting tape to outline a very tiny elongated triangle just above the tree line. Using a sponge or brush, lightly brush over the small opening with clean water and immediately blot with tissue. Do this a few times until the paper appears white again. This is called, *lifting out* color. If the paint is not lifting easily, use a clean toothbrush to scrub the color out. Blot well.

STEP EIGHT

After drying the area and gently removing the tape, emphasize the steeple by adding dark green pine trees using the tip of a small round brush. Then mix a little red with the same dark green to make a warm brown and dot this in under some of the trees near the horizon. Make tiny vertical strokes to indicate the tree trunks.

STEP NINE

Begin at the horizon under the steeple and stroke pale orange across the meadow. Making downward strokes, add purple to the orange near the foreground to create yellow grass in front. Still using downward strokes, add green to the purple mixture going toward the right.

The yellow grass at the bottom appears closer and better defined because of the color behind it.

STEP TEN

After the painting dries, make tiny strokes upward with light and dark green to give detail to the grass. A no. 000 rigger brush is good for this.

STEP ELEVEN

Mix a light Cobalt Blue for the sky. Leave some of the paper dry to create crisp, white clouds. With a clean brush, carefully wash away the blue to soften some of the hard edges. Add a shadow of blue on the right side of the steeple and blue over the yellow grass to make a blue-green.

FINAL

This $1\frac{3}{4}'' \times 2\frac{3}{4}''$ (4.5cm × 7cm) painting can be put into a ready-made mat with the smallest opening and signed on the artwork as shown here.

PROJECT TWO

Putting In

Vary the same landscape by adding foreground trees and lowering the horizon.

Painting Size: 1¾″ × 2¾″ (4.5cm × 7cm)

STEP ONE
Lightly draw the horizon line 1⅛″ (2.9cm) from the top, which is slightly lower than in the previous demonstration. Paint the distant mountain range using a very cool, light gray-violet, similar to the first demonstration. Let the painting dry.

STEP TWO
Mix a slightly darker gray-violet and paint the next mountain range.

STEP THREE
Make sure the paper is dry. Then, as in the previous demonstration, paint the color to the horizon line without diluting with water. This time, just to change the scene a little, dot in light green, forming distant trees. Quickly add dots of yellow-orange in a few places for interest.

STEP FOUR
Begin at the horizon line and with a ¼-inch (6mm) square tip brush, paint orange across the distant meadow. Continue adding a little more yellow and a little more water to the brush, stroking across and down. The result will be a graded wash of orange to light yellow.

STEP FIVE
Use drafting tape to mask out the shape of a steeple and lift the color, just as in Project One. This scene appears brighter because the colors are a little more intense. When blue and orange are mixed together they neutralize each other, but when they are side by side they complement each other. So, if the trees are more blue than green, they stand out more near the orange-yellow meadow. When the paint is dry, add dark blue-green trees near the steeple area with the tip of a small round brush. Gradually lighten going away from the steeple, ending with a very pale blue for the distant trees to the left.

STEP SIX
Paint three pine trees in the meadow, each a different size. They look like they're floating over the meadow now, but adding a shadow will anchor them to the ground.

STEP SEVEN

Add blue-purple shadows under and toward the right of the trees, as if the sun were low and to the distant left. Create the yellow grass in the foreground by painting the shadows behind it with small downward strokes, using only the tip of the brush. Add positive strokes of orange in the foreground grass. The trees repeat the shape of the steeple, and the eye is led to it. The trees also overlap the distant mountain range and give an added feeling of depth.

STEP EIGHT

Deepen the color of the meadow near the horizon line with a glaze of orange. With the tip of a small round brush, dot in green foliage in the grass. Mix a warm brown and make a variety of tiny strokes under the distant trees.

STEP NINE

Use blue with an infinitesimal amount of orange added to it to paint the sky. The tiny bit of orange makes the blue less intense. Cloud strokes go from left to right, pushing the eye in the direction of the steeple, which is the main center of interest. The clouds have both crisp and soft edges.

FINAL

Here is the finished card using an off-white inner mat with a green outer mat.

PROJECT THREE

Putting on a Mask

Use masking fluid to add a path to your landscape. Masking fluid preserves the white paper. It resists water and pigment and can be rubbed off with your fingers or a rubberlike eraser when the area is dry.

Painting Size: 1¾″ × 2¾″ (4.5cm × 7cm)

STEP ONE
Lightly draw the horizon line and path. Wet a small pointed brush with clean water. Remember to work soap into the bristles, using a regular bar of soap or dishwashing liquid, before you apply the masking fluid, so it won't stick to the brush. Paint the mask fluid on the path and the tiny steeple. With the tip of your brush, dot in some masking fluid in the lower left and across the path on the right to reserve some white flowers. Now, paint the distant mountain.

STEP TWO
Paint the second mountain range. It doesn't have to be exactly like the others. Then paint the nearest mountain range, adding dots of yellow-green and yellow-orange while wet. Dry.

STEP THREE
Paint the meadow a light yellow-orange, grading it to light yellow in the foreground. While the paper is wet, add dots of deep pink, green and deeper yellow to the flower area. Dry.

STEP FOUR
Remove the mask by gently rubbing it with your clean fingertips or use a commercial product made especially for lifting mask.

STEP FIVE
Add pine trees in the foreground and background. Use a warm, dark color under the trees in the background and add dark trunks on the pine trees in the foreground.

FINAL
Mix a blue-gray and paint the shadows on the road. When dry, stroke in dark green grass with a no. 000 rigger brush. Use the very tip of your brush in an upward motion and stroke over the shadow and the meadow. Also with the tip of your brush, dot in deep yellow-orange centers in a few flowers to make them daisies. Add a little blue, pink, red and deeper yellow to the flower foliage for variety. Paint the sky with Cobalt Blue. Finally, soften the clouds with a clean, damp brush.

PROJECT FOUR

Wax It

Your landscape becomes a seascape when you turn the meadow into water and add sailboats. We'll use a wax resist method instead of masking fluid to retain the white of the paper in this demonstration. Remember when painting a seascape that water seeks its own level, and large bodies of water don't tilt. Even a large pond or wetland will appear level in the distance.

Painting Size: 1¾" × 2¾" (4.5cm × 7cm)

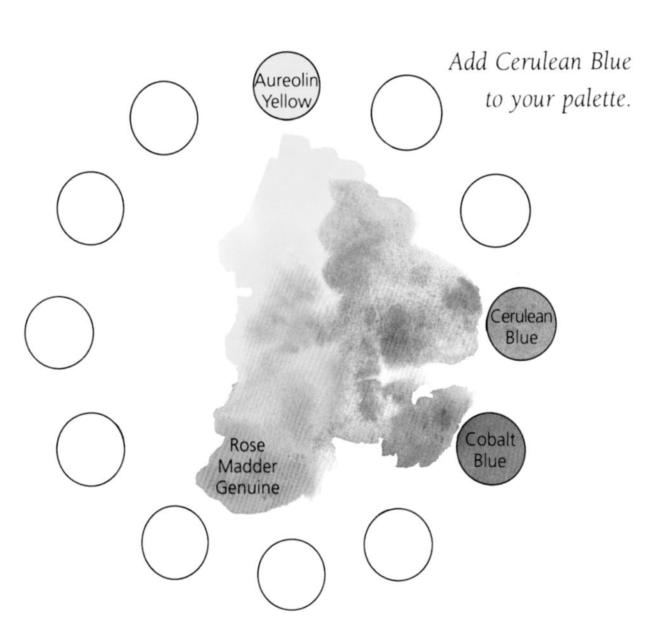

Add Cerulean Blue to your palette.

STEP ONE

Measure 1" from the bottom and mark the tape on both sides. Lay down waxed paper. Using firm pressure, burnish the horizon line with a mechanical pencil or similar tool, but be careful not to cut the waxed paper. Burnish the areas where the sail boats and steeple will be several times. Burnish grasses on the sides of the path so some remain white.

STEP TWO

Using a square tip brush, paint the distant hills with a mixture of Cobalt Blue and red that has a tiny bit of yellow added to tone down the violet. While wet, drop in green and yellow, forming green trees at the shoreline and into the distant hills. Notice that the top of the sailboats, the steeple and the horizon remain white because of the wax resist.

STEP THREE

Paint a graded wash of Cobalt Blue, adding a tint of orange near the water's edge. The water appears lighter and warmer in the shallow area.

STEP FOUR

Mix a grayed violet and paint shadows on the road. When the paper is dry, paint a variety of greens using upward strokes. Before this dries, dab in a little reddish brown, lavender, brighter green and yellow. With just the tip of a no. 000 rigger, stroke in taller grass. Bring strokes of grass over the water to create depth.

STEP FIVE

Use Cobalt Blue, yellow and a touch of red to make a dark green for painting the area around the steeple, the distant trees and the foreground grass. Paint a warm dark under the trees near the shoreline. Stroke in darker grasses with a no. 000 brush.

FINAL

Paint the sky Cerulean Blue, leaving some white clouds and lightening the value toward the hills. Soften the edges of the clouds with a clean damp brush. While the painting is wet, stroke in just the essence of Rose Madder Genuine to warm the area under the clouds and above the hills. You've transformed a landscape into a seascape.

PROJECT FIVE

Straight Up—Using a Vertical Format

The next two projects compare how different the same subject can appear in a vertical format and a horizontal format. Vertical formats convey an attitude of austerity and dignity. Horizontal formats suggest vastness and finality. The shape of the mountain used in these two projects will be familiar to many people—it's the Dome at Yosemite National Park.

Painting Size: 2¾" × 1¾" (7cm × 4.5cm)

Add Ultramarine Blue to your palette. This pigment is slightly granular and has a darker value than Cobalt or Cerulean Blue. It's placed near violet on the color wheel, which means it's a warmer hue. You now have three different blues on your palette: Cobalt, Cerulean and Ultramarine Blue.

STEP ONE
Lightly draw the horizon line and a minimal rendering of the mountain.

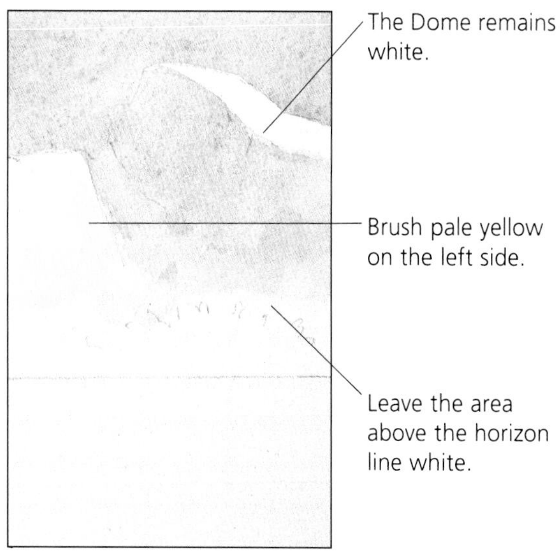

STEP TWO
Paint the sky with a mixture of Cerulean Blue and very little Rose Madder Genuine. Continue painting down into the shadow side of the mountain and lighten toward the horizon line. While the paper is still wet, brush in pink, orange and purple and allow the colors to mingle. Brush a pale, warm yellow on the left side.

STEP THREE
Let the painting dry thoroughly. Mix Ultramarine Blue and subtle mixtures of orange-red and blue-violet to darken areas on the face of the Dome. Mix Cobalt Blue, Rose Madder Genuine and Aureolin Yellow to make a pale gray-green and add tiny trees on either side of the Dome. While the trees on the upper-left side are wet, paint a small triangle of violet under them and let the colors blend. Add diagonal shadows on the left side of mountain.

STEP FOUR
Starting at the top of the painting, paint a graded wash of a fairly bright yellow that lightens to a pale yellow at the bottom. Dry thoroughly. Use wax resist and burnish the tops of the weeds, stems and grass at the bottom.

STEP FIVE
Using dark greenish brown and a downward stroke, paint a thin, straight line to form the trunk of a tree. Add irregular foliage shapes in a light to medium blue-green, letting some of the trunk show. Ultramarine Blue will make a rich dark green when mixed with yellow and a little red; just use less water.

The wax over the yellow resists the dark green painted under the tree. The sun shines from the right in this picture, so the right side of the tree will be lighter than the left.

STEP SIX
Continue painting the trees, making each tree slightly different. Some are yellow-green or blue-green and others are reddish green. These trees are very tall and have huge trunks that must be visible among the foliage. Use tiny downward strokes to create meadow grass. Allow the background color of the mountain to peek through the trees.

FINAL
Mix a variety of warm colors and paint the foreground leaves and twigs. Paint the stems of weeds and add a few dark shadows for contrast.

PROJECT SIX

Low Down—Using a Horizontal Format

Paint the same subject, the Dome, in a horizontal format to give a very different feel to your painting.

Painting Size: 1¾" × 2¾" (4.5cm × 7cm)

STEP ONE

Lightly draw the Dome in a horizontal format.

A NOTE ON COLOR

Beige is basically a yellowish color, but by adding other colors, you can create a green-beige, red-beige, gray-beige, etc. Your beige may be warm or cool, depending on what color you add to it.

Earth colors such as Yellow Ochre, Raw Sienna and Burnt Umber combine all three primary colors, each one in a slightly different proportion.

It takes time to mix these subtle colors, and most artists find it easier to buy them already mixed. For the beginner, however, it's good practice to learn how to mix colors.

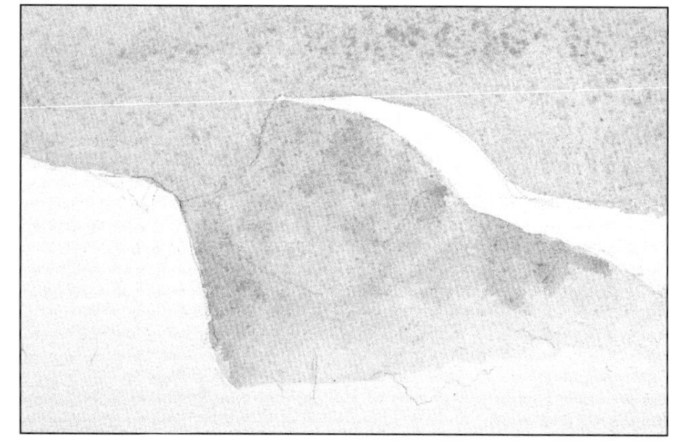

STEP TWO

Paint a light wash of Cerulean Blue and Rose Madder Genuine. Paint down into the shadow side of the mountain. Drop in light mixtures of pink, orange and lavender. Let dry.

STEP THREE

Mix Ultramarine Blue with a little orange to gray down the blue, then darken the left side of the Dome, along the ridge and to the right. Leave the tiny roundish ledge light.

STEP FOUR

Using the tip of your brush, dab in trees on the left side of the mountain with gray-green. Before the paint dries, add a small triangle of lavender and allow the trees and shadow to bleed together. Now add trees to the right side. Stroke in diagonal shadows on the left side. Add pale beige on the Dome.

STEP FIVE

Paint the foreground grass yellow and quickly add Cerulean Blue, Cobalt Blue and Aureolin Yellow.

STEP SIX

When the foreground is dry, use wax resist to keep the meadow grass light. Pull small strokes downward with the tip of your brush to bring out the meadow grass. Paint the tall pine trees, beginning with the trunks and adding foliage. Let the background peek through.

FINAL

Paint a grayed yellow-orange wash across the bottom of the grass to bring out the lighter grass that has wax resist on it. This color will resemble Yellow Ochre.

We often take our surroundings for granted, going through our days without seeing, hearing or feeling the fragile beauty around us. Once we decide to draw or paint a scene, we become aware of what we are actually seeing. Everything becomes more meaningful.

Chapter Three

WHAT A DIFFERENCE A DAY MAKES

A variety of paintings can be created from one scene by just changing the sky, color, season, time of day, size and location. The possibilities are endless.

PROJECT SEVEN

A Change of Color

Create a variety of seascapes with subtle changes in color.

Painting Size: 2" × 3½" (5.1cm × 8.9cm)

Add Winsor Yellow, Winsor Red, Winsor Blue and Winsor Green to your palette.

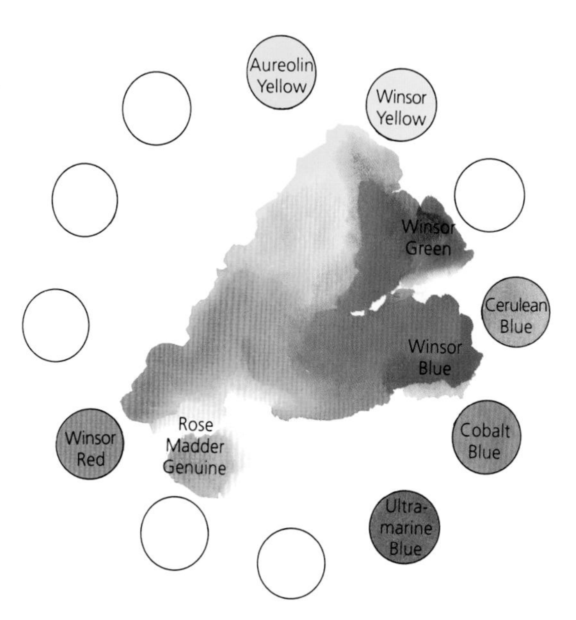

STEP ONE

Draw or trace a simple Sunfish type of boat and a horizon line. Start by making pencil marks on the edge of your drafting tape about ¾" (1.9cm) down from the top of the painting, then line up the horizon with the marks on the tape. Next, tape the tracing paper so that it doesn't move. Trace the boat using transfer paper or rub graphite on the back of your tissue drawing and trace. Replace the graphite paper with waxed paper and burnish the horizon line on either side of the boat. Do not burnish over the sailboat.

STEP TWO

Use Winsor Yellow to paint diagonal stripes on the sail. Let the painting dry thoroughly, and then paint Winsor Red stripes between the yellow ones.

STEP THREE

Paint a flat wash of Cobalt Blue and bring it down to the horizon line. Leave more white above the horizon line on the right side for the beach. While the paint is still wet, drop in light green, orange, yellow and lavender to create trees and foliage. The sky is fairly free of detail. Use a square tip brush to cover the area quickly and cut around the top of the sail.

STEP FOUR

Once the painting is thoroughly dry, erase the transfer lines. With a square tip brush, paint a graded wash of very light Winsor Green down from the horizon, gradually getting lighter toward the shoreline. Carefully cut around the boat. To create the effect of shallow water, stroke a tint of Rose Madder Genuine and Aureolin Yellow across the bottom while the paint is still wet, using the flat, narrow bottom edge of the brush. Leave white paper above the horizon for the beach.

STEP FIVE

When the painting is dry, mix a pale lavender using Cobalt Blue and Rose Madder Genuine and paint over the shallows area. Then mix a little darker tint of Winsor Green and Cobalt Blue and paint across the water near the horizon and boat. Paint the boat blue-gray and add a shadow to the left of its stern.

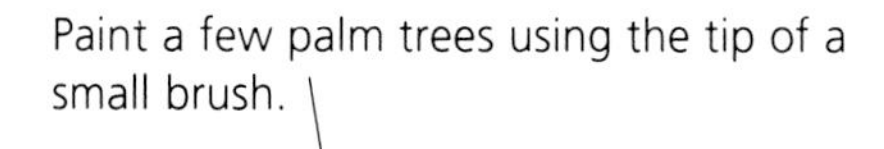

Paint a small stripe of Cobalt Blue above the horizon line.

Paint a few palm trees using the tip of a small brush.

Add tiny distant trees using a pale blue.

Add a tiny dot for the sailor's head.

Add warm darks near the beach foliage.

Paint the stern of the boat a little darker than the rest of the boat.

Put a tiny dab of Winsor Blue in front of the mast to indicate the sailor's shirt. Let the paint dry.

FINAL

Here is the completed painting mounted on a turquoise card that measures 3½" × 5" (8.9cm × 12.7cm).

Change the climate and sail colors for a new look. Add Scarlet Lake, a bright red that resembles Cadmium Red, to your palette.

STEP ONE
Re-use the tracing of the sailboat and use waxed paper to burnish in the horizon line as you did in the last project. This time paint the top of the sail red and the bottom Cobalt Blue. Paint a flat wash from the sky to the horizon using Cobalt Blue with a little Rose Madder Genuine added for warmth. To create the trees, drop in combinations of Scarlet Lake and Aureolin Yellow, Ultramarine Blue and Aureolin Yellow, and Cobalt Blue and Aureolin Yellow. Use pure Cobalt Blue in the land area while it is still wet.

STEP TWO
Paint the water with a graded wash of Ultramarine Blue, adding pale yellow-orange near the bottom. When the paint is dry, add a slightly deeper graded wash of Ultramarine Blue near the distant shoreline. Draw a clean, thirsty brush across the water area to lift out pigment and suggest ripples. Darken and define the trees. Finally, paint an orange shirt on the sailor.

PROJECT EIGHT

The Shadow Knows

The next three paintings make a simple comparison of early morning, afternoon and early evening. When the weather is clear, we can observe the sun changing the landscape as it moves across the sky. The shadows move slowly, but they move, and the direction of the sun determines where the shadows are.

Painting Size: 2¼" × 3¼" (5.7cm × 8.3cm)

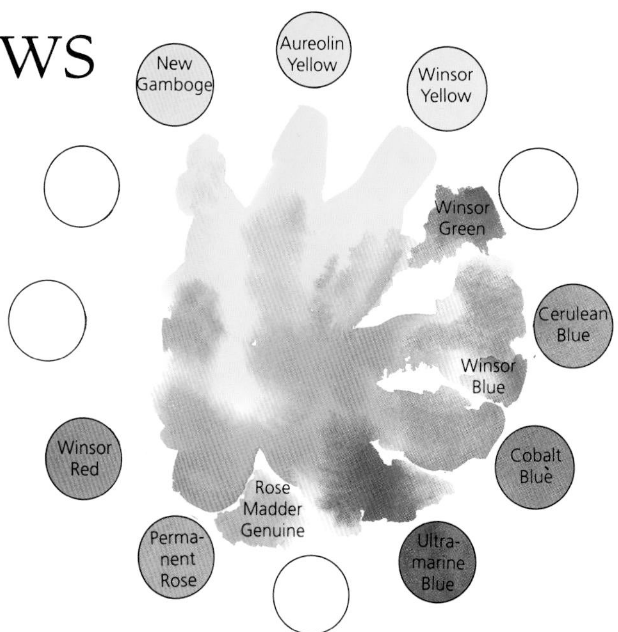

Add Permanent Rose and New Gamboge to your palette.

Early Morning

To begin, reduce the photograph on a photocopy machine to 2¼" × 3¼" (5.7cm × 8.3cm).

Use tissue paper to trace the copy machine reduction. The horizon line must be level and approximately at eye level with the top of the stern.

Measure carefully and mask a 2¼" × 3¼" (5.7cm × 8.3cm) area with drafting tape on your watercolor paper. Make a mark ¾" (1.9cm) up from the bottom on both sides of the tape to show the horizon line placement.

Place the tissue drawing over the watercolor paper and align the horizon with the marks on the tape. Tape the top of the tissue drawing firmly in place so that it will be registered—that is, it will be in the same place each time you reuse it to trace onto the watercolor paper. Keep it taped to the paper so you can flip it up and down until the painting is completed.

This photograph of a boat was taken around midday with the sun overhead. For this demonstration imagine the sun arching across the sky from right to left, not directly overhead, but slightly towards the distant background.

The early morning sun is low on the horizon and rises to the right. That means the right side of the boat will be very light and shadows will be cast to the left. The early sky can be somewhat greenish yellow. Shadows and distant land will tend to be lavender.

Use a photocopy machine to reduce the photograph to 2¼" × 3¼" (5.7cm × 8.3cm).

STEP ONE

Use transfer paper and lightly trace the stern, the right side of the boat and the horizon line. Remove the transfer paper and insert waxed paper. With a mechanical pencil or other smooth pointed instrument, trace the word *Serenity* on the stern, firmly embossing it onto the watercolor paper. Practice on a scrap of watercolor paper to be sure the pressure has embossed the wax onto the paper—when paint is applied, the writing should pop out. Wax resist is a perfect way to keep the boat's name, *Serenity*, white. Burnish the antenna and tiny masts in the distance. Mix Cobalt Blue, Permanent Rose and a little Aureolin Yellow to make a warm gray-violet and paint the stern of the boat. While the paint is still wet, drop in a little yellow near the bottom of the stern to reflect the grass. When the paint is dry, paint masking fluid on the right side of the boat since it remains white. Let the painting dry thoroughly.

STEP TWO

Paint a graded wash of Cerulean Blue to the horizon line. While the wash is still wet, stroke in Winsor Yellow on the right and Permanent Rose on the left. The early morning sky can be quite greenish near the breaking sun. Remember, for this demonstration the sun is rising from the lower right.

STEP THREE

Paint the distant land a grayed lavender. The wax resist masts will appear. Mix Aureolin Yellow and Rose Madder Genuine to make yellow-orange for the beach, then add pale green grass.

STEP FOUR

Trace the rest of the boat and the ladder. Inside the boat use a warm combination of Cobalt Blue, Permanent Rose and Winsor Yellow, which resembles Raw Sienna. Paint a little darker gray-violet under the boat and to the left. Let the painting dry and remove the masking fluid. Paint the shadow cast by the ladder onto the boat.

FINAL
Add more Cerulean Blue to the water. Darken the shadow under the boat. Add the ladder and grasses plus the shadows they cast. With the tip of a small round brush, add highlights below and to the right of each letter of the name *Serenity*.

Afternoon

This demonstration shows the sun higher in the sky, not directly overhead but a little lower and to the left. The top surfaces of the boat catch the light. The boat casts a shadow to the right this time. There's activity on the water and a few clouds are in the sky. The distant land and foreground grass are bright and the sand is very light.

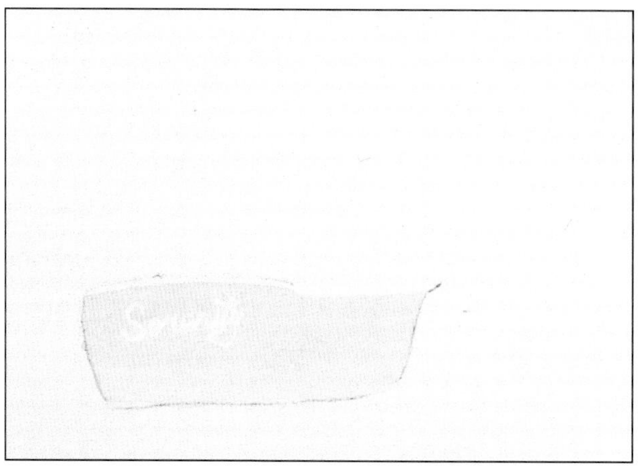

STEP ONE
Set up the same size format, making marks on the tape to line up the horizon. Tape the same tissue drawing to your work. Repeat the wax resist procedure for the name, sailboats and distant shore. The sails will be small triangles because they're in motion. Be sure to burnish well. This time the cabin and top of the deck will be white because the sun is above. Burnish these areas several times. Paint the stern and side of the boat a light blue.

STEP TWO
Leaving some white for clouds, paint a graded wash of Cobalt Blue to the horizon. Add a little orange to neutralize the color at the bottom. Paint the water a darker blue. Mix a light green using Cobalt Blue and Aureolin Yellow plus a little Rose Madder Genuine to gray it down. Paint the distant trees, adding darker green for variety.

STEP THREE
Trace the rest of the boat when the paint is dry. Paint the right side of the boat slightly darker than the stern. Drop in a pale orange near the bottom. Paint the same color orange over the lower stern and wash away with a clean brush above and under the name, so there is no hard edge. Use the same colors for the interior: Cobalt Blue, Rose Madder Genuine and Aureolin Yellow, but mix a warmer color this time by adding more of the red to the mixture.

FINAL
The sun is above and to the left and casts shadows to the right this time.

Evening

There are subtle changes between early morning and noon, but the dramatic change occurs in early evening. In this painting the sun has set but still radiates upward making a colorful backdrop for the scene, which now is in silhouette.

STEP ONE
Place the tracing over watercolor paper that has been measured and masked as in previous demonstrations. Emboss the name *Serenity* onto the paper and very lightly trace the stern of the boat. Wet the sky area and brush in Cobalt Blue, Permanent Rose and Aureolin Yellow, allowing them to mix. Don't overpaint this area; allow the paint to mix itself. Mix a little darker lavender and paint around the stern area. Add blue and continue to bring the color all the way down.

STEP TWO
Be sure the paint is completely dry and then trace everything except the ladder. Paint the distant land dark.

FINAL
The sun has set to the far left. It still radiates, creating its finale of beautiful color in the sky. Everything is in silhouette, so mix a very dark purplish color using Ultramarine Blue, Permanent Rose and a tiny bit of yellow. Paint the boat and beach, leaving a little bluish grass in the foreground. When the paint is dry, lightly wash a little dark over the stern. Once this wash is dry, add the water mark, exhaust hole and sailboat masts and pencil in the antenna.

PROJECT NINE

A Change of Size—Zoom In, Zoom Out

The next four paintings are an exercise in shape, size, season and color. It helps to have a subject with an interesting shape like this barn. It doesn't stand alone but has several other buildings nearby, and I always look forward to seeing it. It's in need of paint and repair, but I feel fortunate on sunny days to look at the shape and see the wonderful shadows on the tower and under the scalloped molding.

A photocopy machine offers an easy shortcut for a seasoned artist or a beginner who wants to paint instead of draw. It's a great tool for enlarging or reducing a photograph for tracing.

Painting Size: 3⅛″ × 2⅛″ (7.9cm × 5.4cm)

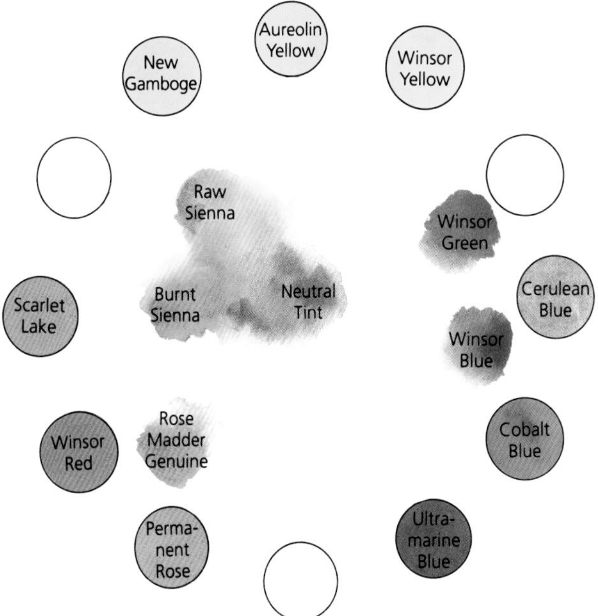

Add Burnt Sienna, Raw Sienna, Neutral Tint and Scarlet Lake. A limited palette forces you to become more disciplined, to push the colors and values to the maximum. It also helps unify a painting by keeping it simple. Using a primary combination of unusual colors such as Raw Sienna for yellow, Burnt Sienna for red, and Cerulean Blue is more challenging and sometimes more interesting. In each exercise I introduce a new technique and more colors. In the second demonstration of this series of four, I introduce a noncolor—Neutral Tint.

The inspiration for the following demonstrations.

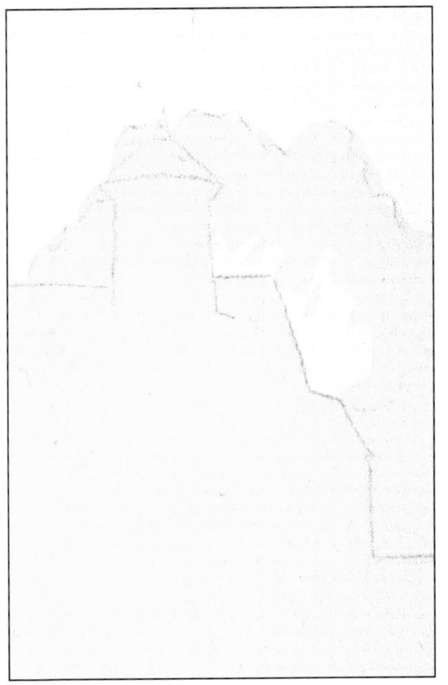

STEP ONE

Use transfer paper to lightly trace the outline of the building and tree onto watercolor paper. Paint a light wash of Raw Sienna on top of the tree. Leave some open areas to fill in with sky color. Continue to bring the color down the building and all the way to the bottom of the painting.

STEP TWO
When the paint is dry, paint a graded wash of Cerulean Blue to the horizon. While this is still wet, create the tree foliage by dropping in Raw Sienna, Burnt Sienna and a green made by mixing Raw Sienna and Cerulean Blue. Drop in Burnt Sienna near the horizon line.

STEP THREE
Retrace the drawing. Use wax resist to make a cross, creating the four windowpanes. Paint the window blue and let it dry. Paint the cast shadow areas on the sunny front of the barn and roof. Mix blue with Burnt Sienna, making a dark brown, and paint in the upper section of the windowpanes and under the tower roof.

STEP FOUR
Begin under the eave on the shadow side of the house and paint down with pale Burnt Sienna. Gradually add blue, combining it with the shadow to the right. Paint the grassy area in front, letting some of the undercolor show. Combine the shadow wash coming down with the grass mound in shadow to the right.

STEP FIVE
Paint dark limbs with a no. 000 rigger. Add foliage. Deepen the Burnt Sienna in the distant trees and make tiny trunk shapes. Paint the green meadow in the distance, leaving a stripe of underpainting to break it up. Add windows and a door on the shady side.

FINAL
Darken the doors and windows. Add the lightning rod with a pencil.

Zoom Out

STEP ONE

Reduce the photograph on a photocopy machine until the barn image is approximately ¾″ (1.9cm) wide. Trace the barn, horizon line, road and weeds on tracing paper. Mark the horizon on the tape ⅞″ (2.2cm) up from the bottom on both sides. Line up these marks with the horizon line on the tracing paper and tape it firmly in place. Wet the sky area with clean water, cutting around the barn carefully so that the sky color won't run into it. Stroke Cerulean Blue, Neutral Tint and a little Burnt Sienna into the sky. Before the paint dries, dot in more Burnt Sienna for the distant trees.

STEP TWO

Mix, then paint Cobalt Blue and Permanent Rose for the shadows on the house and snow. Mix, then paint darker shadow colors for the foreground on the right. While the paper is wet, paint in the grasses with Raw and Burnt Sienna. Add a little Neutral Tint to these colors for darker variations. Neutral Tint looks a little like Payne's Gray, but Payne's Gray is really a dark blue-gray. Neutral Tint is just that—neutral. It doesn't lean in any color direction. Use it to gray or darken a color, but don't overdo it.

A Little Closer

Trace the barn a bit larger on the watercolor paper. We'll create a dramatic fall sunset this time.

STEP ONE

Wet the sky area with clean water, leaving a small area dry to create clouds. Carefully cut around the barn shape. Stroke in Cobalt Blue, Burnt Sienna and Rose Madder Genuine. The white cloud has soft and hard edges. Mix a green using Aureolin Yellow and Cobalt Blue and drop it in near the horizon to create trees. Add purple, pink and other shades of green as well, allowing them to blend without brushing.

STEP TWO

When the paint is dry, trace the details on the barn, trace in the road, and lightly indicate where the foreground weeds will be. Aureolin Yellow, which leans toward orange on the color wheel, is very bright and transparent. Stroke it across the distant field. Mix it with Scarlet Lake, which is also bright and transparent, and paint the roof of the barn.

STEP THREE

Mix Cobalt Blue and Permanent Rose to paint light lavender shadows on the barn and road. Mix New Gamboge and Permanent Rose and paint the left side of the field. While the paper is still wet, drop in deeper pink and green. Paint the window and add a barn door.

STEP FOUR

Mix Winsor Yellow and Cobalt Blue for the light green grasses in the foreground. While the paint is still wet, stroke in pinks, purple and green. Add windows on the shady side of the barn.

FINAL

Darken the sky above the trees to make them stand out, then add trunks to a few of the trees. Add darker green trees with trunks. Allow the background to show through. Darken the shadows in the foreground grasses. Use a deeper pink for the shadows on the barn roof.

Good Night

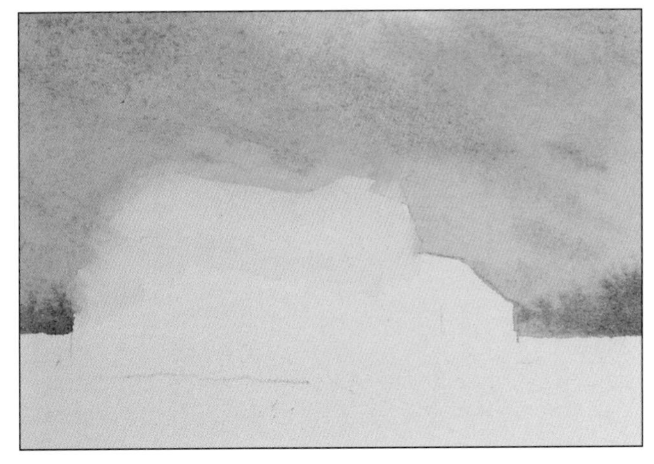

STEP ONE
Trace a copy of the barn that is slightly smaller than the original photograph. Trace only the outline. Place the barn low on the watercolor paper to give more importance to the sky. Wet the sky area to the horizon. This time don't worry about cutting carefully around the barn structure because it'll be painted a dark value. Stroke diagonally from the upper left to the lower right, first with Ultramarine Blue, then Permanent Rose, Aureolin Yellow and a lavender mixture. Work quickly so that the paper doesn't dry. Drop in deep purple at the horizon to make distant trees in silhouette.

STEP TWO
Paint a very pale wash of Winsor Blue over the snow-covered ground. When the paper is dry, bring the tissue tracing of the barn down over the watercolor paper and trace all the details.

STEP THREE
Paint the right side of the barn a light to medium purple-gray. Allow this to dry and then paint a darker shade of purple-gray on the left, including the tower. Add the shadow areas on the snow with a little darker shade. Using a no. 000 rigger, paint the delicate branches of the trees. When the paint is dry, place a piece of white transfer paper under the tissue drawing and retrace details on the barn that were covered with the dark paint.

FINAL
Add windows and shadows over the white tracing. Any white that shows can be erased when the paint is dry.

PROJECT TEN

The Sky's the Limit

Watching the sky is a favorite pastime of mine. If a sky is particularly beautiful or unusual, I'll take mental notes of what I'm actually seeing. For instance: "That top layer of blue is really Cobalt Blue, but near the horizon it looks like Cerulean Blue—and below that, it almost looks greenish gray. The clouds aren't really very white today, they look warm with delicate gray shadows. I think I'd paint a very pale wash of yellow-orange in the cloud area first, but do they have crisp or soft edges? They have soft fuzzy edges, so maybe I'd wash away the edges or—what if I drop the pale color of the clouds onto damp paper. That'll give me the same effect . . ." and so on. The different skies in this demonstration will give you an idea of some of the possibilities.

Painting Size: 2¼" × 3¼" (5.7cm × 8.3cm)

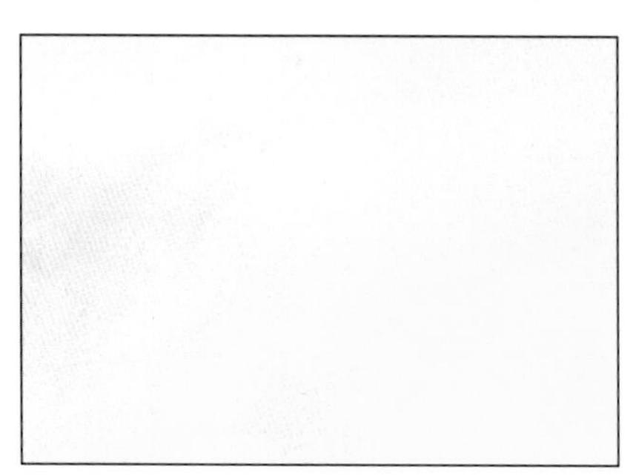

STEP ONE
Paint a very pale wash of Aureolin Yellow, then Rose Madder Genuine, allowing them to mix together in places.

STEP TWO
Define the cloud tops with a pale Cobalt Blue after the wash is thoroughly dry.

STEP THREE
Now use a slightly darker Cobalt Blue and bring the color down on the left side. Add a little of the red to it.

STEP FOUR
Paint the stems of the palm fronds first to give them direction. Some are yellow and others are dark green. The pointed leaves of the palms spread out from the stem but fall in different directions.

FINAL
Add foliage under the palm tree and more palm leaves. Notice that part of the cloud is well defined with crisp edges and soft edges to the left. Even the tiny palm leaves offer an opportunity to provide contrast with color and value.

Another Sky

This demonstration is similar to the first one because the same underpainting colors and technique are used.

STEP ONE
Again, paint a very pale wash of Aureolin Yellow, then Rose Madder Genuine, allowing them to mix together in places. Add a graded wash of violet-gray on the left and down to the horizon.

STEP TWO
This time use a pale Winsor Blue for the sky color, painting around the violet-gray cloud and defining the white clouds behind. While that is drying, paint in water with Cobalt Blue. Pencil in a small sail and the outlines of trees.

FINAL
Paint a small strip of land with a dark mixture of Ultramarine Blue, Rose Madder Genuine and Aureolin Yellow. Don't add too much water to the mixture; it will be quite dark. The overlapping gray cloud adds depth to the sky. The sky color showing between the foliage and the tiny palms also adds to the sense of depth. Although the sailboat is not a pure white, it looks white because of the high contrast.

A Stormy Sky

STEP ONE

This sky is painted with a wet-in-wet technique. Paint from the top down, using Cobalt Blue, slightly washed away, then Ultramarine Blue mixed with Burnt Sienna plus a little Cerulean Blue. Dry this and go back with darker variations of the same colors, leaving the lower part of the sky near the horizon light and painting around the sail.

STEP TWO

One way to achieve a choppy sea like this one is to use a dry-brush technique, in which the pigment grabs only the high spots and skips the shallow craters on the paper. Use the side of a round or square tip brush and gently stroke the paper. Always test on a scrap of watercolor paper beforehand to make sure the brush isn't too wet or too dry. Another way to achieve this effect is to rub white candle wax in an area and then brush over it with color. The wax will resist the pigment, which will go only into the craters.

Two More Skies

Draw a light pencil sketch of the roof lines. The sky is painted wet-in-wet using Cobalt Blue, Neutral Tint, Burnt Sienna and Raw Sienna. Pull the color down to create a path. When this is dry paint the rooftops and trees. To create the snowfall effect, spatter white acrylic paint using a toothbrush.

The contrast between the Cobalt Blue sky and the Winsor Green water places this simple scene in the tropics. Add a billowing cloud over the tiny island and it makes a simple but lovely gift to be framed or placed on a small card.

PROJECT ELEVEN

A Change of Weather

Boaters take advantage of extremely low tides to work on their boats, painting the bottoms or making repairs while the boat is left high and dry on the mud.

Painting Size: 2¾" × 4½" (7cm × 11.4cm)

I took several photographs of a beached lobster boat with its underbelly exposed. That image would make for an interesting painting itself, but I wanted to place the boat on rough water in a way that utilized the camera angle. While Mrs. T *had her bottom scrubbed, I found her a perfect model—she didn't move at all.*

STEP ONE

Trace the beached boat and transfer it to watercolor paper masked off to a 2¾" × 4½" (7cm × 11.4cm) format. Use wax resist for the antennas and paint masking fluid on the entire boat except the windows. Also mask the wave crest in front of the boat, a few white caps and the buoys.

STEP TWO

When the mask is dry, paint the sky and water all at once. Begin at the top and quickly stroke in Cerulean Blue, then Cobalt Blue all the way down. Immediately go back and add diagonal strokes of Neutral Tint and Raw Sienna near the horizon as well as in the foreground area.

STEP THREE

When the art is completely dry, remove the mask. Put the tissue drawing back over the artwork and trace the water mark on the boat. Paint Scarlet Lake on the exposed bottom of the rolling boat. Put a tiny red blob inside the cabin to represent a lobsterman's jacket.

STEP FOUR

Paint the stern of the boat with Raw Sienna to the water line. Mix Raw Sienna with a little Scarlet Lake and paint reflected light inside on the cabin roof. Mix Burnt Sienna with a little blue to make a warm dark brown and paint the two portholes, the bottom of the boat that is in shadow, and inside the cabin where it shows through the window. Paint a small dot for the fisherman's head. Paint a light blue shadow from bow to stern along the transom and between the two stern colors. Mix a darker blue and add detail to the water in the foreground.

FINAL

Paint the buoys. Use a sharp pencil to lightly define the antennas. Notice that the bow of the boat is reflected in the water. Lightly pencil in the right sides of the antennas. Notice the reflection of the bow on the cresting wave. Pencil in the boat's name, *Mrs. T*, on the stern. Notice that the buoys all point in different directions.

PROJECT TWELVE

A Docked Lobster Boat

Painting Size: 2¾" × 4½" (7cm × 11.4cm)

The boat Bridgit *had just docked, with spring lines secured, when I took this photo. The harbor dock provides a safe haven when the seas are running high. Exercising my artistic liberty, I left out a lot of detail and simplified the buildings. The red of the foul-weather suit is repeated on the house trim, the barrel and the boat's water line. The angles of the boom and spring lines break up the horizontal thrust of the painting.*

STEP ONE

Trace the photo of the docked lobster boat and copy it onto a piece of masked off watercolor paper. Use wax resist for the spring line ropes from the boat to the dock. Burnish the tiny rope lines with the back, dull side of a pocketknife. Press firmly but not enough to cut through the paper. Paint masking fluid on the boat, the man on the ladder, the house on the right, and a couple of crates on the dock.

STEP TWO

Mix a light warm gray using Rose Madder Genuine, Cerulean Blue and Aureolin Yellow. Paint the whole format except the nearest white house. Rectangles are easy to paint around using a square-tipped brush.

STEP THREE

Mix a slightly darker green-blue gray and paint around the shed on the left side of the house. Drop in a little darker version of the gray mixture to simulate the distant trees. Paint the right side the same color, leaving the underpainting for the left side of the small house.

STEP FOUR

When the paper is dry, trace the reflection in the water. Paint the dock a warm tan using Raw Sienna and a little Scarlet Lake on the dock side. Add a greenish blue-gray going down into the water. Paint around the reflection with irregular strokes using the narrow side of the brush. The masking fluid looks dirty because it's picking up the transfer paper. This won't affect the painting when the mask is removed.

STEP FIVE

Trace the pilings and then paint the negative shapes between the pilings with a blue-green gray.

STEP SIX

Before removing the mask, define the huge rocks by painting between them with a warm brown. Dry the artwork thoroughly and remove the mask. Paint a very light and warm glaze of yellow over the boat hull and the house.

STEP SEVEN

Trace details on the house and boat. Paint the lobsterman Scarlet Lake Red and the doors, shutters and bottom of the boat a slightly lighter tint. Paint the porthole dark.

STEP EIGHT

Add more trees near the house. Paint the lobster traps and cans. Mix a darker red and define shadows on the man, the door and the red can. Mix a dark green to paint the water around the reflection. Bring some of the dark green up into the pilings. When the paper is dry, mix a warm dark brown and paint between the bases of the pilings and into the water on either side of the piling reflections.

Repeat of the angle on the left side of the dock.

Red accents are repeated on the man, house, the barrel and at the water line.

The man ascending the ladder brings life to a very still setting.

Repeat of the angle in front of the distant house.

Notice how the angle breaks up the monotony of the strong horizontal motif.

FINAL

Notice that the spring lines on the boat filled in somewhat with pigment. To make them light again, take the point of a penknife or the tip of a razor blade and gently go over the lines. Because there is wax underneath, the paint will scrape off easily.

What have you got to lose? Go ahead and paint small works of art. A small area of white paper is not very intimidating. If a painting has not evolved the way you want, just go on to another without losing much time and expense.

Chapter Four

MADE TO ORDER

Alter the color scheme, size and shape of a subject to fit a specific card, mat or frame. A two-dimensional painting can become three dimensional. There are no limits to the interesting choices you can create.

PROJECT THIRTEEN

When Colors Scheme

Photographs capture my interest. How I use the information in the photographs is the creative part. Rearranging a composition and color scheme to fit a particular card is a great exercise. For instance, if I want to use blue and turquoise cards, I introduce these colors in the background to coordinate with the cards.

Painting Size: 3⅝" × 2⅛" (9.2cm × 5.4cm)

This photo is nice, but I can alter the color and create a lovely color scheme to match cards I want to use.

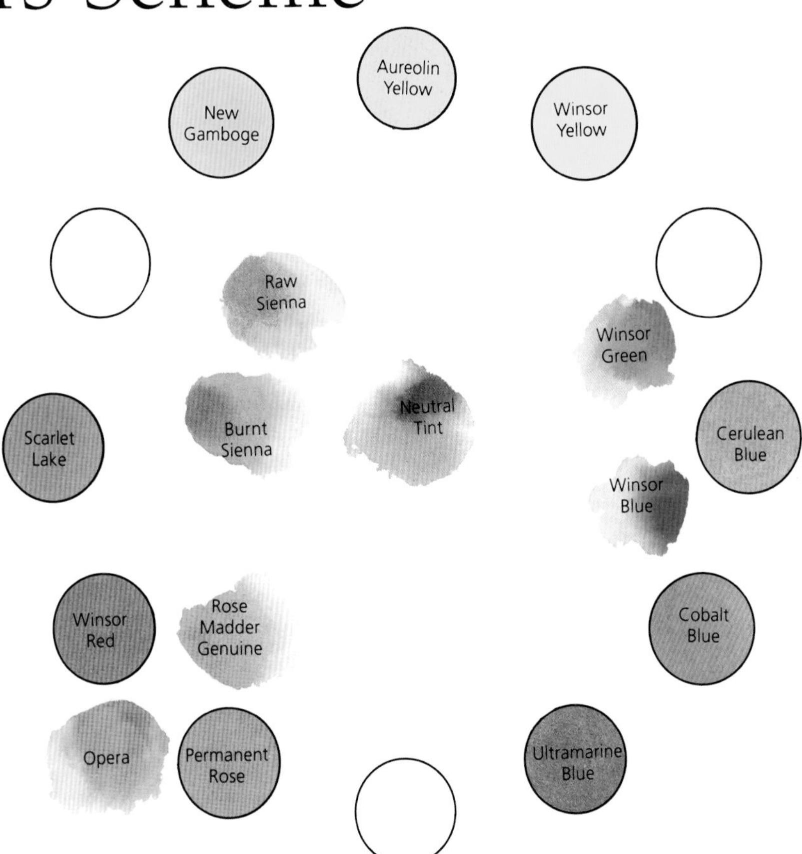

Most of the watercolor tube paints I use are made by Winsor & Newton, but I use some made by other manufacturers as well. For instance, Opera by Holbein is introduced in this demonstration. Opera is an incredibly intense red. It's a fugitive color, which means that it will lose some of its intensity over time, but I still use it—it's outrageous! Manufacturers make some colors that we can't mix ourselves. Look at color charts displayed in art stores and note the interesting violets, purples and mauves. Combining warm blues and cool reds, such as Permanent Rose, Rose Madder Genuine, Opera, etc., will make nice violets or purples, but the tube colors are much brighter.

When Colors Scheme

STEP ONE
Draw a rectangle on tracing paper that is the same size as the format opening, $3\frac{5}{8}'' \times 2\frac{1}{8}''$ (9.2cm × 5.4cm). Place it over the photo and trace flowers one at a time, rearranging them to improve the composition. Tape the finished tracing over the format opening and trace onto watercolor paper.

STEP TWO
Paint the petals and bud using Opera mixed with a little Cobalt Blue. Add a little bit of New Gamboge to the top of the bud.

STEP THREE
When the paper is dry, use a darker purple-pink, adding just a tiny bit of yellow to gray it down, to create shadows and to separate petals.

STEP FOUR
Paint the flower centers with a mixture of Opera and New Gamboge to make bright orange. While the paint is still wet, drop in a little Burnt Sienna on the right sides of the cone centers. Mix a light warm green and paint the stems and leaves. Let the paper dry; erase the pencil lines.

STEP FIVE

Mix Burnt Sienna and Ultramarine Blue to make a rich, warm dark. Using the tip of your brush, make tiny dots near the top of the cone heads and fill in the nearest petals. Bring the dark down between some of the petals, creating a scalloped effect. Mix a dark warm green and paint the right side of stems, the cast shadows, and on some leaves.

STEP SIX

Mix enough Cobalt Blue in a medium tint and paint the background. The only section that requires quick painting to cut around the flowers is at the top. All other small negative spaces are contained by the edge, petals, leaves and stems.

I tailored the completed painting for this blue card.

PROJECT FOURTEEN

Still Life of Daffodils

Although the abundant flowers in this white bucket were worth photographing, the shadows caught my eye. The only whites on what appears to be a white bucket are the flecks of light filtering through the flowers from the skylight above. White isn't always white, especially when the cast shadow on the table is very close in value to the bucket.

Painting Size: 3⅝" × 2¼" (9.2cm × 5.4cm)
Card Size: 3⅝" × 2⅛" (9.2cm × 5.4cm)

STEP ONE
Draw a border on tracing paper to fit the dimensions of the card the painting will be mounted on. The photo is horizontal, but I chose to use the card vertically. Orient the tracing paper format vertically over the photo and move it around until the composition is satisfactory. Make sure the bucket is not tilted. Look for interesting negative shapes around the subject. Trace and transfer onto watercolor paper that has been masked to size.

STEP TWO
To maintain the white areas, brush masking fluid on some of the petals, flecks of white on the bucket, the handle and the light spots on the table. Remember to soap the brush before dipping it into the masking fluid and wash it promptly when you're finished.

STEP THREE
Paint the flower area with Winsor Yellow first. Quickly drop Aureolin and New Gamboge Yellows intermittently. Each yellow is slightly different. While still wet, drop in orange centers in several flowers with a mixture of Scarlet Lake and New Gamboge. Paint a graded wash of Winsor Yellow on the bucket, gradually adding a little New Gamboge Yellow near the bottom on the table and the basket area.

STEP FOUR
When the paper is dry, paint a light mixture of Permanent Rose and Ultramarine Blue over the bucket, basket and down into the shadow. Immediately add a darker mixture to the left side of the bucket and the shadow area. Also paint the violets and dot in yellow centers with the tip of your brush. Dry thoroughly and remove the masking fluid. The dry yellow underpainting on the bucket neutralizes the lavender wash on top.

STEP FIVE

Paint the remaining white areas with a light to medium value of Winsor Green that matches the card, including around the violets and in between a few daffodils. Let the paper dry. Paint the basket orange and mix a darker blue-green to define the violet leaves. Paint small flecks of light in the shadow on the table with New Gamboge.

STEP SIX

Be sure the surface is dry and place the tracing back over the work. Trace the bucket handle and shadow. Mix a very dark value of green with Winsor Green and Scarlet Lake. Paint between the stems and add a few darks in the daffodils and violet leaves. Paint cast shadows on top of the bucket with darker blue-lavender. When this is dry, paint the wire handle very dark. Mix a red-orange with Scarlet Lake and New Gamboge and add a little Cobalt Blue to resemble Burnt Sienna. Paint alternate dashes around the basket. You can use Burnt Sienna for this, but it's good to practice color mixing.

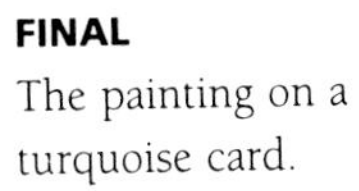

FINAL

The painting on a turquoise card.

PROJECT FIFTEEN

Copy Cat

The process of creating and painting is a special time for any artist, but painting one hundred of the same Christmas or Hanukkah cards is boring. Color copiers now reproduce art work very close to the original, which provides an inexpensive way to reproduce art and opens the door to opportunities that were cost prohibitive and time consuming in the past.

In this demonstration we'll paint four different ski scenes to fit a card or letterhead that measures 8½″ (21.6cm) across. Then make color copies, separate and glue onto cards or letters. The originals can be framed or given as special gifts. These paintings brought back fond memories for me, but if I had to paint one hundred of them, I don't think my enthusiasm would last.

Painting Size: 2″ × 6½″ (5.1cm × 16.5cm)
With ⅜″ (1cm) border, 2¾″ × 7¼″ (7cm × 18.4cm)

Cut a piece of watercolor paper 11″ × 7½″ (27.9cm × 19.1cm). Use masking tape to attach the paper to your board. Cover ⅜″ (1cm) of the paper on all four sides with tape, which creates a white border on the card. There should be 6½″ (16.5cm) of paper showing from left to right. Use a square angle or a piece of paper to make sure the area inside the tape is square and accurate. Measure down from the inside of the top tape 2″ (5.1cm) on both sides and draw a light line across. Measure down ¾″ (1.9cm) on both sides and draw a light line across. Continue measuring until there are four areas that measure 2″ × 6½″ (5.1cm × 16.5cm) with ¾″ (1.9cm) space between.

STEP ONE

Now tape the format 2″ (5.1cm) down from the top, creating the first card area to paint. Begin with a mixture of Cerulean Blue and a little Rose Madder Genuine and paint the sky, distant mountain and shadows on the snow.

STEP TWO

Dry the work and paint the distant trees a pale blue-green. I use the bottom edge of a small square tip brush to make the treelike shapes. Paint them quickly. The top edge of the distant tree area is ragged; its curved bottom edge defines the slope. Let dry and paint a darker gray-green for closer trees. Notice that the bottom of the foreground tree trunks are placed in an irregular pattern, which creates distance. The trees are darker in front with small tree tips sticking out of the snow.

STEP THREE
Continue adding trees. Be sure to leave a path between the trees for a skier. Add the skier.

STEP FOUR
Now add a flag and the other skiers. They are barely defined in the distance. Use white gouache and spatter with a toothbrush to create snow.

STEP FIVE
When the paper is dry, mask a second painting area below, leaving ¾" (1.9cm) between the formats. Lightly draw mountains and figures. Paint the sky Cobalt Blue and the distant land a blue-green gray. Foreground shadows are made with Cobalt Blue and Rose Madder Genuine.

STEP SIX
Add skiers and light blue-green trees. This time use pencil to make the ski poles.

STEP SEVEN

Add tiny dots for skiers far down the mountain on the lower left. Cover the top of the painting with a paper towel and spritz blue-white on the snow area with a toothbrush to give the snow the appearance of being tossed by the skis and poles.

STEP EIGHT

Mask off the next area below. Draw a snow ridge, trees and skiers. Paint the sky Cobalt Blue and allow the blue to define shadows in the foreground trees. Paint skiers in deep powder with snow cover up to their knees.

STEP NINE

Paint large trees leaving white and blue shadows on the snow-covered branches. Paint distant skiers and trees. The squiggles of ski marks pull both sides together.

▸

STEP TEN

Mask off another area below and lightly pencil in the trails and skiers. Paint distant trees a light blue-green and the foreground trees a little darker. Notice the white trail on the left peeks through the trees. The skiers get very small toward the background. Two figures coming up the trail add depth because only their torsos show. Spatter with white gouache.

Here are the finished products, cut apart and glued on colorful cards.

PROJECT SIXTEEN

Love Your Anemones

I always look for new ideas for cards and gifts and unusual ways to present paintings. I noticed one of those plastic cubes usually used for photographs in the photography store and decided to use it for a three-dimensional painting instead. The cube comes apart so you can trace the pattern inside the cube onto watercolor paper to make an unusual three-dimensional gift.

The subject can be almost anything. You could wrap a landscape or seascape around the cube with clouds on top. I was inspired by a gardening book when I opened it to a page full of anemones, my favorite spring flowers. "Love Your Anemones" popped into my mind and made me laugh, and so I thought it might make someone else do the same.

Painting Size: 3″ (7.6cm) squares
Completed Work: Six 3″ (7.6cm) squares

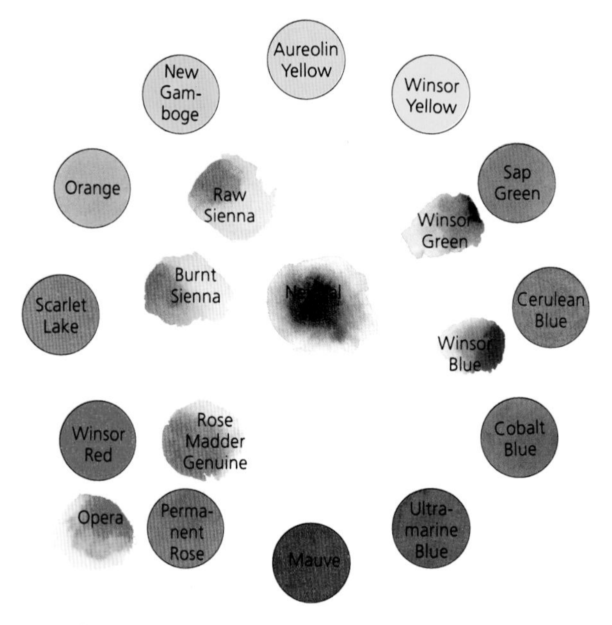

Introduce mauve and Sap Green to your palette.

This is what the finished product will look like before it is inserted in the cube. The pattern resembles a cross. When it is scored or embossed along the lines, it becomes easy to fold.

PHOTOGRAPH BY MIKE RICHTER

STEP ONE

Open the cube and remove the cardboard. Place the pattern on a half sheet of watercolor paper and trace lightly. Tape the work to a table or board. Mask off and work on one square at a time. Lightly draw the flower. Wet the center with clean water and paint around the edges, allowing the paint to dilute itself into the wet center. Use Scarlet Lake, which is a nice bright red. Don't rush; stop halfway around. Dry the paper and when ready, re-wet the center and continue painting around the petals.

STEP TWO
The drawing is still visible. To define the petals stroke a little darker red along the edge of the petal and quickly wash away the outside edge. The petal pops out without being outlined. This technique is called *lost and found*.

STEP THREE
Continue defining petals and add some tiny lines in each one. Have a very good photograph to work from or have the real thing in front of you. Add dark Winsor Red to the center, and when the paper is dry, dot in very dark purple centers, allowing some of the red to show through. The foliage of anemones is unique, and a few leaves set the flower off.

STEP FOUR
Painting a white anemone is tricky: How do you make a white flower stand out on white paper? Use the lost and found technique and it becomes simple. Lightly draw the flower. Mix a *very* pale blue-gray and outline about 1" (2.5cm) at a time around the outside of the flower. Immediately wash away the outside edge with clean water. This takes time, but the results are worth the effort. You can also use the side loading technique.

STEP FIVE
Mix a light blue-lavender gray and define the interior of the petals as well as the edges.

STEP SIX

Let the paper dry thoroughly. Wet the center of the flower with clean water and stoke outward with radiating lines. Drop in the purple-violet center and allow the paint to bleed out into the wet lines that radiate from the center.

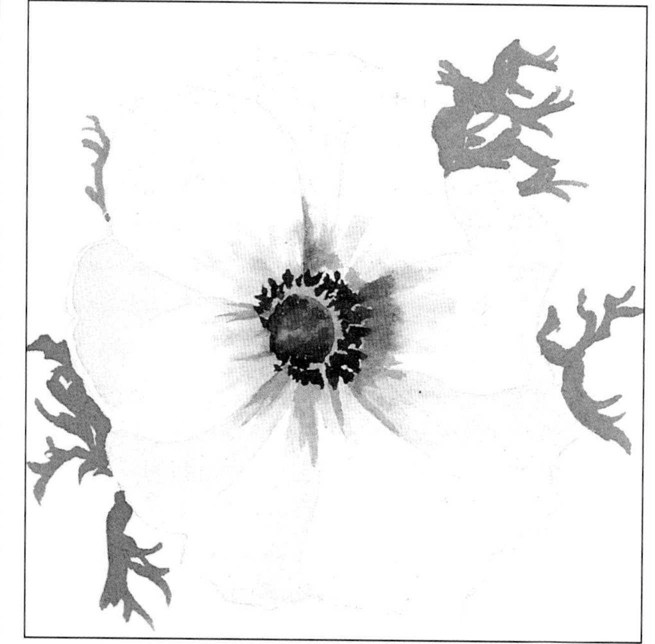

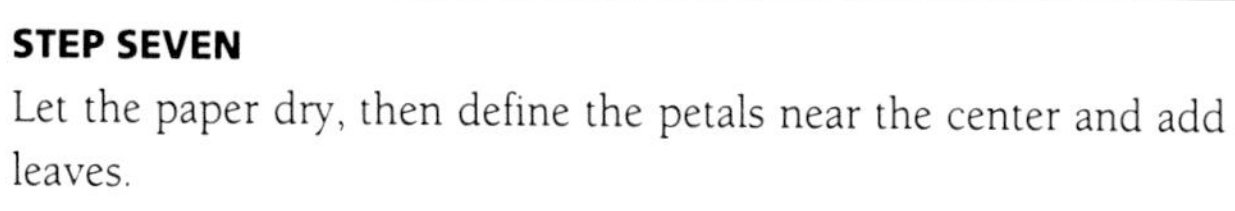

STEP SEVEN

Let the paper dry, then define the petals near the center and add leaves.

STEP EIGHT

For the pink anemone use Permanent Rose and paint the whole blossom the same color. Some of the petals are lighter near the edge. Use lifting out to remove some of the pigment. To lift out color, go back with a clean, *thirsty* brush and lift off the pigment. You may have to do this several times. (See chapter one for more detail on this technique.) Define the petals; add the center and leaves.

STEP NINE

Paint the purple anemone as you did the pink blossom. Mauve has been added to the palette, but you could mix it with Ultramarine Blue and Permanent Rose to create a nice purple-violet.

STEP TEN

In the square that will be on the top of the cube, lightly letter "Love Your Anemones." Paint masking fluid over the letters. When it is dry, wet the area in random patches and drop in color, allowing it to blend. Let the paper dry and remove the mask. Below and to the right of each letter, highlight with a darker undercolor to accentuate.

STEP ELEVEN

The bottom of the cube is for the message. Paint a small bud and write your message.

STEP TWELVE

Laid flat, the painting looks like a cross. Lightly mark where the folds are on the front of the work. Use a ruler as a guide and score, applying firm pressure with the back edge of a dull knife. This makes it easier to fold the paper.

PHOTOGRAPH BY MIKE RICHTER

Completed painting in a plastic cube.

PHOTOGRAPH BY MIKE RICHTER

PROJECT SEVENTEEN

Stretch It

One day at the camera store an unusual plastic frame caught my eye. It was designed to hold a panoramic photo that measures 3¼″ × 10″ (8.9cm × 25.4cm). I thought it would be a nice display for an elongated painting. It's molded to stand on its own, and artwork can be slipped in the side opening. It makes a perfect desk, shelf or tabletop display. An original painting inside makes it a simple and elegant gift.

Painting Size: 2¾″ × 9¼″ (7cm × 23.5cm)
Framed Size: 3½″ × 10″ (8.9cm × 25.4cm) with ⅜″ (1cm) border

STEP ONE
Measure 1¼″ (3.2cm) up from bottom and lightly draw a horizon line, rocks, boats, beach and distant land. The sky will seem a long way across—don't try to do it all at once. Notice that I wash the pigment away on the right side of the sky. On location, the wind dries the paper quickly. In the studio, I use a dryer. The sky colors are Cobalt Blue and Cerulean Blue mixed with a little Rose Madder Genuine near the horizon. Paint around the tiny sailboats.

STEP TWO
Continue painting the sky from left to right, washing the right side away each time. If the paint is washed away properly, no unwanted brushstrokes will show. Darken the sky near the horizon line to give more contrast to the sail, using Cobalt Blue and Neutral Tint.

STEP THREE
Paint the distant land. To give more dimension, drop in other colors to give the land an interesting form. Add light gray rocks using Neutral Tint. While the paper is wet, drop in other light colors.

STEP FOUR

Paint the water in stages to keep it manageable. Mix Winsor Blue and Winsor Green to make a light turquoise. While waiting for the water to dry, paint the beach with Yellow Ochre down into the shallow part of the water, adding a little lavender for shadows.

STEP FIVE

Continue painting the water, leaving white paper for waves and gradually getting lighter toward the shoreline. Define rocks and paint different greens for foliage.

FINAL

The completed painting. Notice how little the foliage is defined. The overall shape of the different colors defines the foliage without painting a lot of detail. Add some shadows to the water.

Completed work in plastic frame. PHOTOGRAPH BY MIKE RICHTER

Disasters sometimes happen on large or small paintings. Going back to a not-so-good painting gives you the freedom to explore new techniques and see it from a different perspective. The process is more important than the product.

Chapter Five

ONE THING LEADS TO ANOTHER

Consider all the possibilities—a subject can be painted many ways: One idea may lead to another, opening many creative doors.

PROJECT EIGHTEEN

A Wee Drop

I placed a beautiful, overripe pear in front of me and did a freehand drawing. The pear's shape is subtle and so is its color. I automatically dipped my brush in Sap Green and added a little yellow, because I thought a pear is green. I tested the color. Wrong! The pear is yellow with a little green added and a blush of red. Because it's so ripe, there are many brown spots and scars—the perfect ripeness to model its voluptuous shape and, like a weathered face, more interesting to paint.

After you've practiced you'll be able to paint a pear without much of the glazing demonstrated here; however, it's a good technique to master and allows you plenty of time to make decisions. You must know when to stop glazing and dry the work thoroughly before continuing. Practice is the best teacher.

Painting Size: 4½" × 3½" (11.4cm × 8.9cm)

A NOTE ON COLOR

Use a staining color, such as one of the Winsors, as the local base color if several glazes are to be added. Permanent, staining colors are strong enough to show through, and they don't lift off as easily as nonstaining pigments.

STEP ONE

Make a freehand drawing of a pear. Add slightly different sized circles with masking fluid for the water droplets. If you're working with an actual pear, dip your brush into clean water and sprinkle a few drops on the pear to see where they stay. Dry the mask thoroughly and paint the whole pear Winsor Yellow. Immediately brush in Yellow Ochre mixed with Sap Green on the sides and Winsor Red and yellow in the center. Paint the stem a light value of Burnt Sienna with a little Neutral Tint added.

STEP TWO

Darken the stem. Paint the left, shadowed side of the pear a mixture of Sap Green, Yellow Ochre and Neutral Tint. Wash away pigment toward the center to give an undefined curve to the pear.

STEP THREE

Deepen the red in the center and wash away the edges. Quickly add Yellow Ochre, Aureolin Yellow and Sap Green. Lift out the soft highlights in the upper center with a thirsty brush. There are no hard edges within the pear shape.

STEP FOUR

Darken the left side a little more. Add Raw Sienna on top around the stem. Mix Raw Sienna and Burnt Sienna and paint the scars and tiny dots. Let dry and remove the masking fluid.

FINAL

The secret of painting a water drop is the highlight and the shadow. Paint the color of the top drop similar to the color that surrounds it but *leave the highlight white*. If the light source is from the right, then the highlight will be on the right side of the drop. When the paint is dry, add a tiny curved shadow around the left side. One of the droplets is slightly elliptical. To make the pear sit down, add a lavender-yellow gray shadow to the left. The background, defining the table edge, is barely seen and is washed away toward the top.

PROJECT NINETEEN

Inside the Big Apple

Painting Size: 5″ × 5″ (12.7cm × 12.7cm)

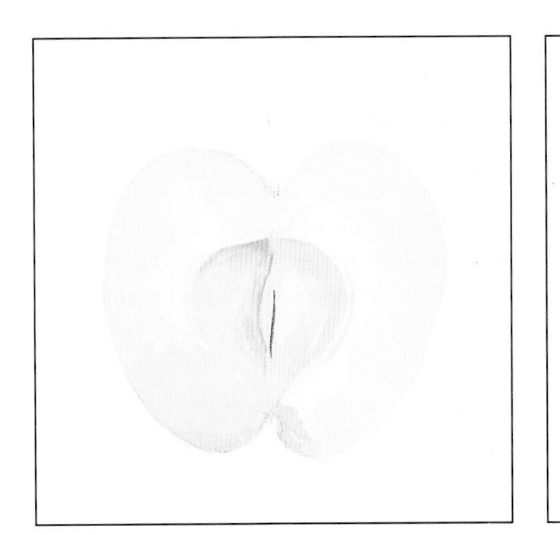

STEP ONE
Make a freehand drawing of an apple sliced in half. Paint a very pale wash of Winsor Yellow and very little Sap Green on the interior, leaving white areas.

STEP TWO
The left side of the apple has cool reflected light at the top. Paint the left side with a cool red mixed with a little green. Wash away the edge to the right so no brush marks will show under additional glazes. With a very small brush, stroke around the left side with red; define underneath the apple, seed, stem and interior.

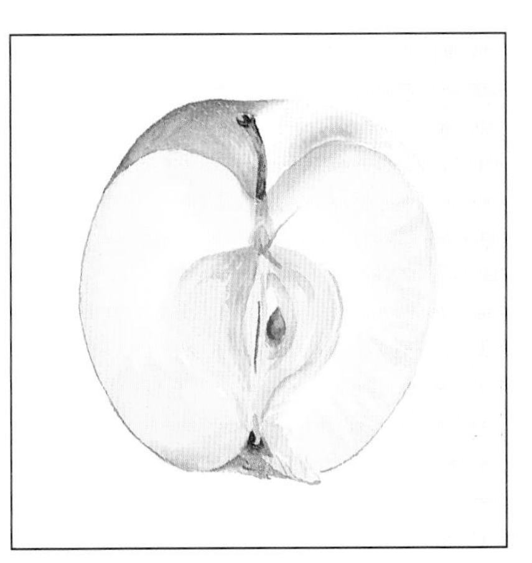

STEP THREE
Add a soft-edged cool red to the upper right. Use a Scarlet Lake glaze on the left, leaving a cool highlight. Dry. With the tip of a tiny brush, dot in Naples Yellow on the left side. Add a shadow under the base of the apple.

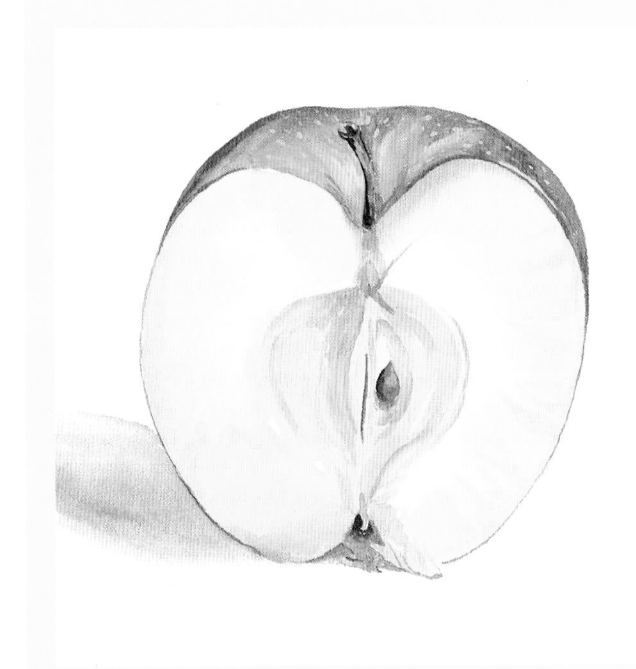

FINAL
Add green to the upper center and define the edge. Notice the small strip of highlight along the cut edge. Use Winsor Green with Scarlet Lake dropped in for the shadow. Notice the tiny dots and dashes have direction emerging from the center.

PROJECT TWENTY

Hard Rocks

"I can't paint rocks," said one of my students. "Mine all look like potatoes." She was piling one oval (potato) rock on top of another and there was no feeling of depth. We all have pre-conceived ideas of what a rock *should* look like. Even when working from a photograph of rocks, that pre-conceived idea influences how we really see the rock.

Try turning the photograph or painting upside down. It's an excellent way to confuse the noisy and interfering left brain and keep it out of the process. Let the right brain take over and ask, What shape is this thing? What angle am I seeing in relation to the other lines? What color is this? Is this bigger or smaller than the thing on the left? Are these bright or muted colors? Is it a smooth shape? Does it have texture and sharp edges or do the edges melt away?

When I was artist-in-residence at Yosemite National Park I took pictures of wildflowers called Scarlet Gilia. They were against a rock ledge and the sun shone on them. I've used that subject six times in six different paintings, with several different techniques and mediums. No two were alike.

For this demonstration, put the flowers in front of an interesting rock formation. These rocks are hard-edged, angular and cracked.

Painting Size: 2¾″ × 4½″ (7cm × 11.4cm)

STEP ONE

Make a freehand drawing on tracing paper and then trace it onto watercolor paper. Make tiny dots with liquid mask for the Scarlet Gilia, which will be painted bright red later. Let the paper dry. Remember, there's no one way of painting anything. I point out what I did and the colors I used so the reader can follow along, but this is not the only way to achieve the end result. Go ahead and experiment.

STEP TWO

Use Cerulean Blue for the sky. While the paint is still damp, lift out the tree trunks with a thirsty brush. Mix blue with Neutral Tint and paint the slate-looking rocks. Go back and stroke a light Burnt Sienna on the trees.

STEP THREE

The whole lower section is painted all at once. Burnt Sienna, Raw Sienna, Aureolin Yellow, Rose Madder Genuine, Neutral Tint and blue are brushed or dotted in and allowed to mingle. Dry and retrace if necessary.

STEP FOUR

Paint the top rock with Burnt Sienna, Raw Sienna and Neutral Tint. While the paint is slightly damp, sprinkle a little salt in that area. While waiting for that to dry, define the lower section. Paint a variety of greens around the top rock and drop in darker green for shadow in the lower area.

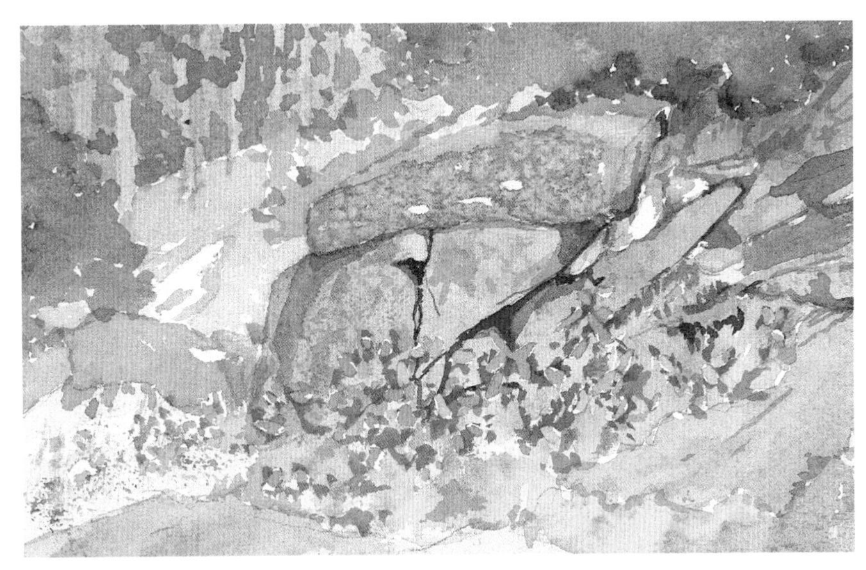

STEP FIVE

Paint several shades of green in the tree area, letting some sky peak through. Add greens around the flowers. Dry thoroughly and paint the flowers a bright red.

FINAL
Continue to define rocks, grasses and trees. Make dark shadows on the trees. Each trunk is broken up with color. Notice the direction of brushstrokes under the bushes. Use a dry brush on the slate.

Hard Rocks Another Way—A Different Technique for the Same Subject

STEP ONE
Here's the same scene using a different technique. Lightly trace the drawing onto watercolor paper. Paint the whole area wet-in-wet, loosely following the drawing underneath. Use Cobalt Blue, Rose Madder Genuine, Aureolin Yellow, Winsor Green, Burnt Sienna and Scarlet Lake.

FINAL
This painting is defined much like before and resembles the other painting, but it has another feeling.

PROJECT TWENTY-ONE

Soft Rocks

This demonstration shows the well-worn rocks along the coast of Maine. They've been sculpted into soft, sensuous shapes by the relentless force of nature.

Painting Size: 2¾″ × 4½″ (7cm × 11.4cm)

STEP ONE
Make a freehand drawing indicating the horizon line and the angle of the rocks. Paint the rock area wet-in-wet with Yellow Ochre, Burnt Sienna, Ultramarine Blue and Rose Madder Genuine. Trees are only indicated with vertical lines.

STEP TWO
Use Cerulean Blue for the sky with a little Rose Madder Genuine added near the horizon. While the sky is still wet, drop in some light green near the rocks to give a soft look to the bushes. Dry and paint the distant land a lavender made with Ultramarine Blue and Rose Madder Genuine. Dry the painting. Add trees, letting the sky peek through near the tops. Define the round edges of the foreground rocks with light washes of Burnt Sienna and Scarlet Lake. Paint the rocks on the right, defining them with a dark brown. Dry brush the lower rock in the foreground with a lavender-blue gray.

FINAL
Add detail to the trees and distant rocks. Paint a gray-green where the water has discolored the rocks with algae near the water line. The rocks in the background are softly defined. The trunks of the trees are not painted all the way. The boughs hide some of the trunks. Sharply define the shadow under the foreground slab. Dry brush in the foreground.

PROJECT TWENTY-TWO

Coastal Rocks in the Fog

Painting Size: $2\frac{3}{4}'' \times 4\frac{1}{4}''$ (7cm × 11.4cm)

STEP ONE
Lightly draw the horizon line and indicate the slope of a rock slab. Paint a Cerulean Blue and Rose Madder Genuine graded wash down to the rock slope. Dry thoroughly and add blue-green treetops. Wash the bottom.

STEP TWO
Leaving the light area under the trees white, add a very light lavender and Raw Sienna mixture down to the rock slope. Dry and define nearby rocks with a slightly darker variation of the same color.

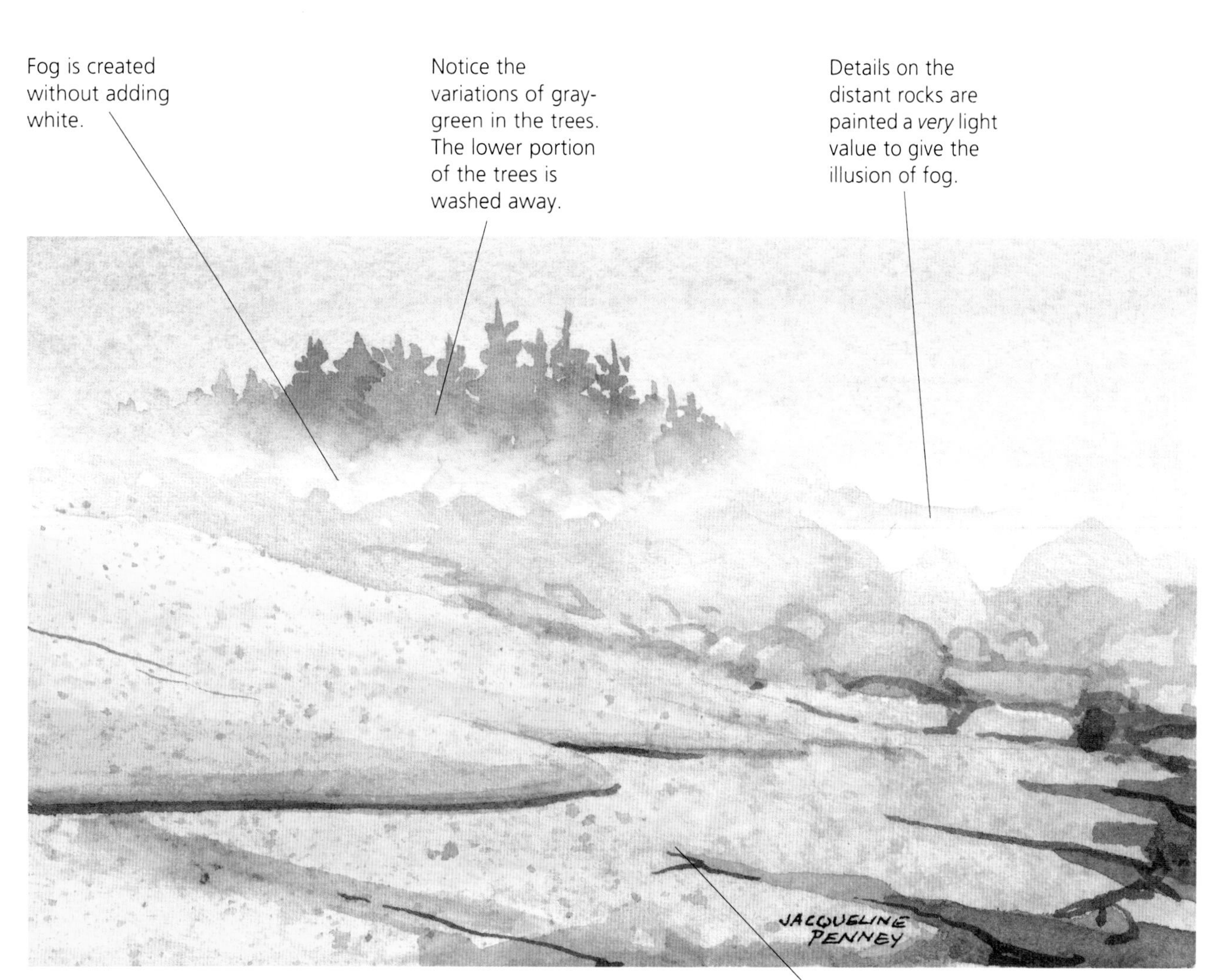

FINAL
Paint a light to medium wash of Yellow Ochre on the sloping rock in the foreground. Let the paper dry. Cover the upper part of the painting, then spritz the rock with several different light beiges and grays. Let dry and add detail.

PROJECT TWENTY-THREE

Little Rocks

In this demonstration I chose to paint the small rocks I see along the rocky coast of the Long Island Sound on the North Fork. They are little gems that sparkle in the sun.

Painting Size: 2¾" × 4½" (7cm × 11.4cm)

Here is a photo of the Little Rocks *setup.*

STEP ONE

Set up a still life of rocks and shells. Draw lightly onto watercolor paper.

STEP TWO

Mask the shells and areas of rock to remain white. Dry the mask and paint one rock at a time, so that each rock is different. Skylight from overhead creates dull highlights on the smooth rocks. Pull out the highlights with a thirsty brush while the paint is still wet. Create the roundness of the stone by painting around the edge with a slightly darker value and allowing it to blend with the rock color.

STEP THREE

Continue adding rocks one at a time. The striated rock in the upper right is painted with Neutral Tint. However, many beautiful grays can be mixed using colors that are already on your palette. The piece of weathered beach glass is painted with a combination of Winsor Green and Neutral Tint.

STEP FOUR
Remove the mask on the right side. Lightly define the shells and rocks with pencil.

STEP FIVE
Paint inside the scallop shell with a *very* pale lavender and leave white highlight. Paint the left scallop shell a pale yellow.

STEP SIX
Paint details on the shells and add more rocks.

FINAL
The completed painting.

PROJECT TWENTY-FOUR

Have a Seat

Painting "what isn't" is a right-brain pleasure. It forces you into a different way of seeing, a new mode of operation.

When you concentrate on a negative shape, your eye is drawn into that space. For example, when you focus on the space between the arms of an Adirondack chair, you no longer see the chair. The mind may say, put flowers or a field of grass behind the chair. Once the painting starts, however, there's a release of responsibility to create "something."

I enlarged photographs of Adirondack chairs in the photocopy machine to fit the format I wanted. The tracing of these chairs can be used over and over again to create different scenes and explore techniques and colors.

Painting Size: 2¾" × 4½" (7cm × 11.4cm)

STEP ONE

Place a tracing of Adirondack chairs over watercolor paper that has been masked to a format of 2¾" × 4½" (7cm × 11.4cm). Tape the tracing securely to your board above the painting area. Trace the outline of the chairs including the space between the arms, seat and back. Don't worry about the slats yet.

STEP TWO

Use Scarlet Lake to paint irregular blobs for flowers in the negative shape of the chairs and also to the right and above. Add Sap Green mixed with Raw Sienna and paint below the flower shapes to make leaves. Fill in the whole space to the edge of the outline. This negative space creates the armrest, seat, back and front leg without painting them. The areas to the right and above form the rest of the leg and arm.

STEP THREE

Add more flower buds made with Aureolin Yellow and Scarlet Lake mixed to make a bright orange. Add New Gamboge and a little of the orange and paint the flowers to the right.

STEP FOUR

For a change, use Permanent Rose on the left and a different hue of red. Add Winsor Green and Raw Sienna to make the leaves. To cool the garden down a bit, add Cobalt Blue above the orange flowers and blue mixed with red to make lavender flowers to the right above the yellow flowers.

STEP FIVE

Paint around the flowers mixing different greens as you go: Winsor Green mixed with New Gamboge; Sap Green mixed with Winsor Yellow; Ultramarine Blue mixed with Aureolin Yellow; and so on.

STEP SIX

Make mounds of blue-green and pale green behind the chair on the left. While the paper is still wet, sprinkle a little salt in the area. Allow this to dry slowly for about five or ten minutes. It gives the effect of lighter buds or leaves. Paint a pale gray-green under the chairs, making negative grass shapes at the bottom. Notice how the chairs seem to pop out.

STEP SEVEN

While you wait for the salt to be absorbed, paint more grass in the foreground, mixing several different greens to make it interesting.

STEP EIGHT

Paint the sky Cerulean Blue. While this area is wet, dot in lavenders, blues and yellow over the blue on the left. The diffused color gives the impression of distance. Fill in more dark greens for accent and warm brown on the right to resemble earth.

STEP NINE

Let the painting dry. Place the tracing back over your work. Trace the detail on the chairs. If the sun is from the right, the left side of the chair will be in shadow. Mix a light lavender and paint the shadows on the chair. Notice that background color is painted in between the slats rather than just a shadow color.

FINAL

Continue painting the chair on the left, adding shadows and details. Dry and erase the lines.

PROJECT TWENTY-FIVE

Adirondack Chairs Facing Out

Painting Size: 2¾" × 4½" (7cm × 11.4cm)

STEP ONE

Trace an enlargement of the chairs facing out, then retrace onto the watercolor paper. This time mask out all of the chairs. Dip a toothbrush in soapy solution, then into a small amount of masking fluid. Using your finger, spritz the mask over the entire work surface. Be sure to place paper towels around the area so that the mask doesn't get onto anything else.

STEP TWO

When the mask is dry, paint pale yellow, orange, pink and blue over all. Dry the paint and spritz masking fluid over all again. Dry.

STEP THREE

Trace a shadow on the watercolor paper. Paint it with a mixture of Ultramarine Blue and Scarlet Lake. Let the painting dry.

STEP FOUR

Paint the grass in the distance (at the top of the painting) with a pale green and blue-green. Make uneven downward strokes to create the closer grass area.

STEP FIVE

Continue painting the grass using different greens. Dry thoroughly and remove mask.

STEP SIX

Trace the details on the chair. Mask out between the slats. Paint light blue shadows on the chair. Oops! I forgot to mask out the front leg on the right chair. No problem. Put drafting tape on either side and lift out.

FINAL

Make the shadows deeper on the back rungs and legs. Add the shadow on the left. Put in stems and paint some of the flowers pink and orange.

You can truly experience a place by sketching and painting on location. Take it all in: the sights, the sounds, the smells and the feelings. Original postcards are a nice reminder of where you've been and a thoughtful gift for friends.

Chapter Six

POSTCARD POSSIBILITIES

A postcard provides a variety of formats for creative paintings to send to friends or to keep as a pictorial travelogue.

Blank postcards on 140-lb, (300g/m²) cold press watercolor paper come packaged in pads and can be purchased in art supply stores. The pads are compact and easy to pack for travel. It's less expensive, however, to make your own. One sheet of watercolor paper will make twenty-five cards. They'll save money and work as well as ready-made cards.

Painting postcards on location or even from photographs you take on vacation is an ideal way to capture the mood of a place. You can paint lovely scenes in different formats to send to friends or to keep as mementos with notes written on the back.

Postcards let you interpret a location or subject in many ways. You can turn your head in any direction and the view changes. Look closely for objects that relate to the scene or gaze off in the distance for a wide expansive view. Notice a small architectural motif or a weed growing through the cracks of a stone walkway. There are no limits to the subject matter and format sizes you can use. Land or seascapes, a field of flowers, a bouquet or single flower. You could use objects on a table in a little café or sketch people as they sit and eat. Use your imagination!

Here are some possible formats.

The formats don't have to be perfect or even outlined. The eight rectangles shown here may be a place to paint interesting doorways or windows; cups from different restaurants; flowers; and so on.

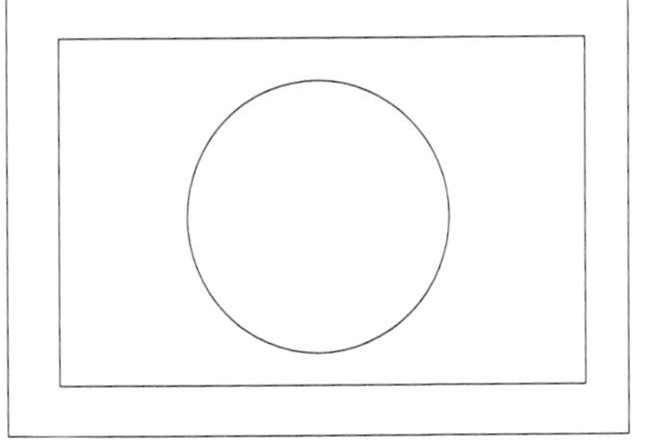

Use a compass or a glass to make a circle. The less perfect the more personal and appreciated it seems. It can be the world with an arrow pointing to where you are or hold a flower, a design, a country's name.

Vertical formats offer many possibilities: a building, door, window, flower, tree, bridge, or standing person. Horizontal formats may hold a landscape, seascape, bench, low bridge, etc.

Paint a colorful, decorative border to set off your written note inside the frame.

Three slightly different horizontals can be filled with parading birds, interesting signs, a string of laundry, a train.

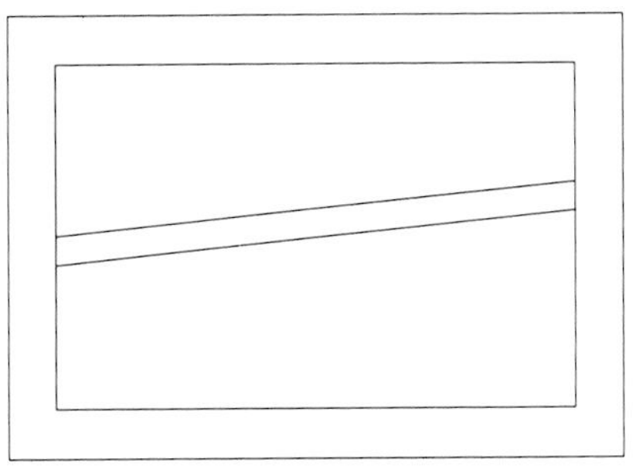

Nothing has to be equal. Dissect the card any way that pleases you or that sets off what you want to paint.

PROJECT TWENTY-SIX

Three Beach Scenes on a Postcard

Postcard Size: 4″ × 5¾″ (10.2cm × 14.6cm)

STEP ONE

Tape ¼″ (6mm) around the postcard. Measure down 1½″ (3.8cm) and tape across. Lightly pencil in the horizon line ½″ (1.3cm) from the top of the tape.

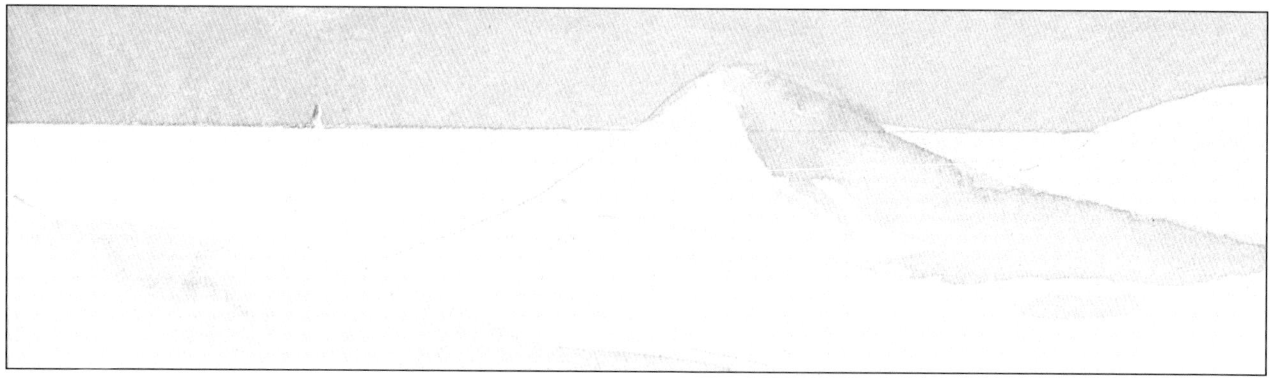

STEP TWO

Wax resist a sail. Lightly draw in dunes. The light source is from the left. Paint the sky Cobalt Blue. Add a tiny bit of Rose Madder Genuine and paint the right side of the dune. Use an even lighter wash in the left foreground.

STEP THREE

Dry and erase the lines on the dunes. Paint the water with a pale to light wash of Winsor Green. Add a little orange near the foreground while it is still wet.

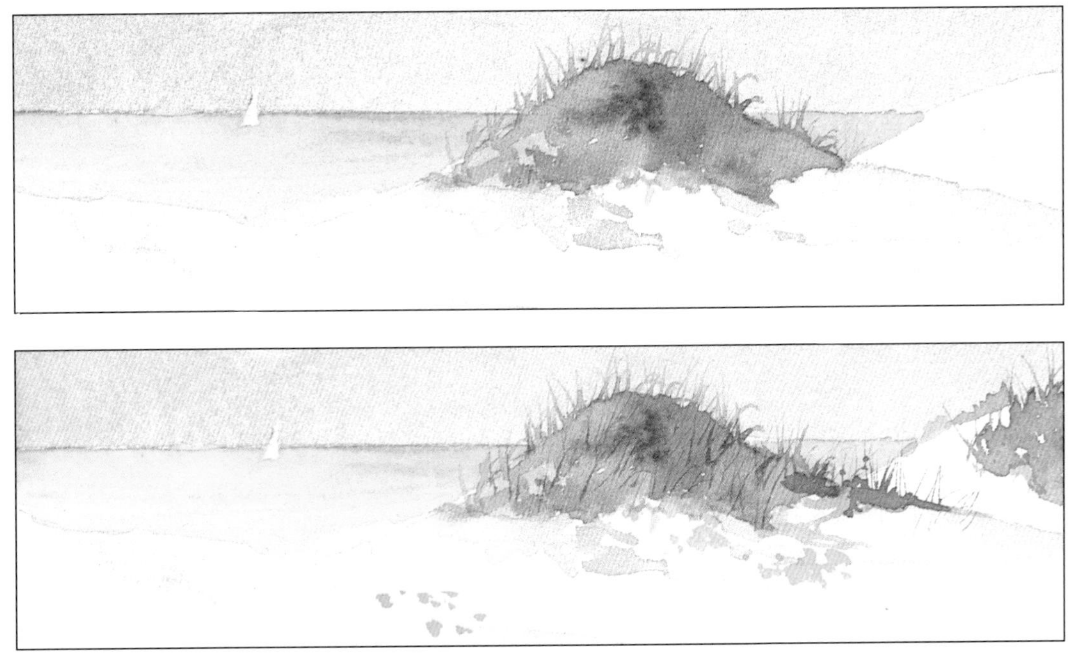

STEP FOUR

Paint the dune with Sap Green and New Gamboge. Add blue to the right side and dot with lavender and yellow. While the paint is wet, pull up thin grasses with a no. 000 rigger.

STEP FIVE

With the tip of your brush, dab Aureolin Yellow for dune daisies. Use several different greens and paint the right side of the dune, dragging up with a no. 000 rigger to make the grass higher. Bringing the grass up to overlap the water and farthest dune gives the impression of depth.

STEP SIX

Paint the left dune grasses darker. Notice the lavender-gray shadows on the sand. Surround the yellow daisies with green.

STEP SEVEN

Dry the painting thoroughly. Now bring the masking tape up ¼" (6mm) and press down again. Add a vertical strip of tape on the right to make a 1⅝" × 1⅝" (4.1cm × 4.1cm) square on the right.

STEP EIGHT

Paint a smaller version of the same scene. Make clouds and leave out the daisies.

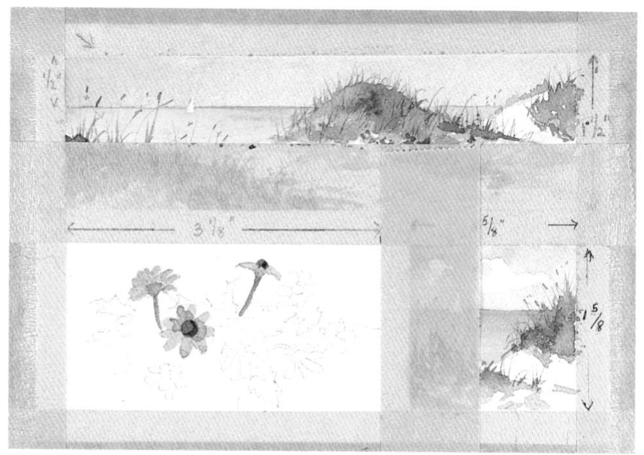

STEP NINE

Re-tape the lower left square and lightly draw the yellow and white daisies. Use New Gamboge and Aureolin Yellow for the daisies and, when they are dry, Burnt Sienna for the centers. Notice that they are not all facing the same direction. Add the two stems.

STEP TEN

Mix Cobalt Blue and Rose Madder Genuine into a light blue-lavender and paint the sky. Cut around the white daisies and add more yellow ones.

STEP ELEVEN

Paint Sap Green around the flowers. Drop in different greens.

STEP TWELVE

Dry and add dark green accents. Pull up some grasses with a no. 000 rigger.

The completed postcard.

PROJECT TWENTY-SEVEN

Another Postcard Possibility

Here's another subject that will make people smile. I no longer hang out my wash, but in our rural countryside I often see laundry on the line drying in the breeze. The variety of subjects to paint is endless. Even this one subject changes with the shape of the clothes, sheets, towels, etc., hanging on the line.

Postcard Size: 4″ × 5¾″ (10.2cm × 14.6cm)

STEP ONE

Lightly draw the clothes and tree. Wax resist the clothesline wrapped around tree trunk and the tiny clothespins. Paint the sky, leaving white paper for clouds. Under the clothesline, paint greens around the laundry. Paint the tree and grass. When dry, paint the clothes.

STEP TWO

Let the painting dry, then move the tape down to leave ¼″ (6mm) between the lower left section and the top painting. (There is a ¼″ border separating them.) Add a strip of tape on the right. Lightly draw the basket and paint the sky and shadows on white laundry. Dry the work between each step. Paint the basket, clothes and grass.

FINAL

Here is the final card. To complete the last painting move the vertical strip of tape and leave ¼″ (6mm) between the basket and the new section. Draw a close-up view of the line and pins. Paint the sky around them. Paint under the clothesline and down between the two pieces of laundry. Add details.

PROJECT TWENTY-EIGHT

Three in One—Three Views of Maine

I sat on a Maine island rock and painted the three views you see on this postcard. By just turning my head slightly, I could take in a vast area. Each view has a different light source and the sky and water change very quickly.

Postcard Size: 4″ × 5¾″ (10.2cm × 14.6cm)

STEP ONE

Mask off an area 1¼″ (3.2cm) down from the tape indicating the horizon line or eye level. Lightly draw in your subject. Paint the sky Cobalt Blue, leaving puffs of white clouds. Paint around a tiny house.

The water is a mixture of Cobalt Blue and Neutral Tint; the distant land is a gray-lavender. Leave a white space between the water and land for a rocky shoreline.

STEP TWO

Paint Yellow Ochre on the foreground rocks and, while wet, add Burnt Sienna to soften the shape. Paint the grass and bushes on the island with light green; add a little darker green accent. Paint the rocks Yellow Ochre.

STEP THREE

Add trees on the left, bringing the green down into the rock crevices. Add darks between the rocks. Define the distant island rocks. The light is directly overhead. Add shadows on the house. Use masking tape to make a tiny sail and lift out gently with a sponge and tissue. Dry.

STEP FOUR

Mask off a vertical rectangle 2" × 1¾" (5.1cm × 4.5cm) on the right side of the card. Lightly draw rocks and green bushes. Paint the sky a graded Cerulean Blue wash down to the bushes. Paint the rocks Yellow Ochre and Burnt Sienna near the bottom. Add a little green to show low tide marks. Dry, then paint green bushes.

STEP FIVE

Paint the spruce trees. Darken the greens. Add cracks in the rocks.

STEP SIX

Mask the left side of your card leaving ¼" (6mm) space between paintings. Wax resist the gulls. Paint a very light wash of Cobalt Blue and Rose Madder Genuine down to the horizon line. Make the sky slightly darker near the bottom so the sea gulls show. While waiting for that to dry, paint the rocks a light value of Burnt Sienna and Ultramarine Blue and then darken the rocks near the water. Make sure the area is dry before painting the water in the foreground.

STEP SEVEN

Mix a light blue-gray green for distant trees on the left going into a violet-gray to push the tiny trees farther away. The water is a light Cobalt Blue. Add trees on the island and detail on the rocks. Add green sea grass and reflections. Use dry brush on the large rocks in the foreground.

The completed postcard.

PROJECT TWENTY-NINE

A Different Angle

This daisy postcard is masked off in angular formats to show a different way to cut up a rectangle. There are so many ways to make a card more interesting that don't take much time and are fun besides!

Postcard Size: 4" × 5¾" (10.2cm × 14.6cm)

STEP ONE

Tape ¼" (6mm) around the postcard. Angle your tape across and use another piece going down to create an angular shape. Lightly draw two daisies and one bud. Paint shadows on the daisies with Cobalt Blue and Rose Madder Genuine along with a touch of Aureolin Yellow to gray it down. Paint Cobalt Blue around the daisies. Paint the daisy centers Aureolin Yellow and add Yellow Ochre around the sides. Paint the stems and leaves yellow. The blue underneath will turn the yellow into green. When this is dry, darken the stems and leaves. Add a light lavender on the centers for shadows.

STEP TWO

Lift off the tape carefully and replace the top one to leave a ¼" (6mm) between formats. Lightly draw the daisy contours; the shapes they make when clumped together as well as singly. Paint these daisies the same way but paint more of them and make them smaller. Use the same blue to paint around the upper daisies. Drop in a little green on the right.

STEP THREE

Add yellow centers but don't place them all exactly in the center, which would make all the daisies seem to face forward. Add green to the lower portion.

STEP FOUR
Add negative darks to bring out the positive stems and leaves.

STEP FIVE
When the painting is dry, lift the tape and place it up a ¼" (6mm). Add another piece of tape on the left side, leaving a border of ¼" (6mm). Use a wet-in-wet technique beginning with a pale blue-lavender wash. Leave some areas white. Add yellow, orange, pink and lavender. Let the paint dry and add centers to the flowers.

FINAL
Add more colors and darker greens and your card is finished.

Many of my most creative paintings have evolved from "rejects." Try to find a use for projects that didn't work out whether they're large or small. Tear them, cut them, weave them into a collage. Scrub them and use the paper again. Use part of them for a card, place setting or gift tag.

Chapter Seven

LETTING GO

Allow watercolor to drip, blend and flow without interference—it stimulates your imagination and brings out your creative spirit. Without expectations come wonderful surprises.

PROJECT THIRTY

When Paint Runs Into a Sky

Many of the projects so far have been fairly structured. Let's loosen up and let the watercolor do more work.

Painting skies is the perfect time to let the pigments run together. The austere trees in this painting emphasize the winter sky. This little painting reminds me of a wonderful quote by Anthony deMello: "Love the plant in winter when it says nothing."

Painting Size: 3¾" × 2⅛" (9.5cm × 5.4cm)
Card Size: 5¾" × 4⅛" (14.6cm × 10.5cm)

STEP ONE
Start with Cerulean Blue at the top. Use irregular strokes to add Neutral Tint and combinations of the two. The sky is not all one value or one color. Add a little Raw Sienna near the bottom. Keep the snowy hill on the left dry to create a crisp edge. On the right, create shadows on the snow by bringing the lower sky color down.

STEP TWO
Paint the trunks of the trees with Burnt Sienna and Neutral Tint using the edge of a ½-inch (12mm) square tip brush. Overlapping strokes create the appearance of bark or shadows. Paint the tiny branches with a small round tip. Notice the broken angles of the branches. Add grasses using combinations of Raw and Burnt Sienna mixed with Neutral Tint.

FINAL
The completed card. The presentation of the little paintings in the "When Paint Runs" projects is unique. The blank cards are made in Germany but can be duplicated as well. A rectangle is cut out for the art and embossed around the edge to give it the effect of a frame. The art is slipped in behind the opening. The card's a trifold so the back of the artwork is covered on the inside. They come in a multitude of colors and sizes and have matching envelopes.

PROJECT THIRTY-ONE

When Paint Runs Into a Flower

I looked at a seed catalog and created my own rose plant for this project. The finished painting looks crisp, but the paint was allowed to run together in a contained area.

Painting Size: 3¾" × 2⅛" (9.5cm × 5.4cm)
Card size: 5¾" × 4⅛" (14.6cm × 10.5cm)

STEP ONE
Paint a light tint of Rose Madder Genuine into irregular shapes that resemble petals but are not defined. Quickly add a little darker mixture of the same color. Add Scarlet Lake to give some brightness. Paint everything while the underpaint is still wet. Add Sap Green leaves under the rose shape. Apply Burnt Sienna with a tiny brush for the tips of the leaves. Mix Sap Green with yellow for the stems and with Cerulean Blue for the leaves. Notice that each leaf is slightly different in shape, value and color.

STEP TWO
Repeat the same process but place the second rose slightly behind the first. Add New Gamboge yellow to its center. Add leaves. One even stands alone, unattached.

STEP THREE
Paint the rosebud with Permanent Rose and add more yellow. Notice that an inverted wishbone shape has emerged. This stem is darker than the others. Add leaves.

FINAL

Paint the last rose a paler pink to keep it in the background. The last stem is fairly straight. All four stems and roses are slightly different, which makes for a more interesting subject. The pale pinks and yellows are complemented by a pale green card.

OR . . .

You might choose a bolder color like this magenta.

PROJECT THIRTY-TWO

When Paint Runs Into a Bouquet

Painting Size: 3¾" × 2⅛" (9.5cm × 5.4cm)
Card Size: 5¾" × 4⅛" (14.6cm × 10.5cm)

STEP ONE

When you want to include crisp white flowers in a bouquet using the wet-in-wet technique, the paper in that area needs to be dry. It's important for your colors to be moist in your palette. The small areas dry quickly and can't wait for you to scrub the dried paint with water to loosen it up. Begin with Winsor Yellow, then New Gamboge right next to it, then Scarlet Lake, then Opera. These colors are all dropped into a ¼" (6mm) area that forms the top flower(s). Continue adding color: Ultramarine Blue, Cobalt Blue, Winsor Green, Raw Sienna. Notice the two white areas in the middle of all that color.

STEP TWO

Continue adding colors. Although the bouquet colors are pastel, there is still a wide range of value, adding interest.

STEP THREE

Lightly draw a cylindrical container that is slightly off center to the right and show where the flowers will end. Notice the interesting negative shapes. Add flowers sticking up on the top right of the bouquet.

STEP FOUR

Continue adding colors, leaving white paper for the white flowers. Add more leaf shapes near the bottom. Add yellow and blue flowers sticking out a little on the left.

FINAL

Paint the container Cobalt Blue, lighter on the left and darker to the right. Add more darks in the bouquet and around a few leaves.

PROJECT THIRTY-THREE

When Drips Drop

Splashing paint on a wet or partially wet piece of watercolor paper is just plain fun, and it's surprising what interesting colors and shapes emerge. Many times when I just don't feel like painting "something," I paint "nothing." When I allow myself some fun and creativity, I find that it's a good idea to have no expectations. However, it's a rare day that something doesn't emerge from this exercise. Many of the greeting cards I send to friends come from my splashing around, letting the color do it's thing. A child can manage this fun exercise with a little guidance and create invitations to a party, Valentine's Day cards, birthday cards or thank you notes.

Work on a level surface for this technique and keep the paper flat so the colors can run evenly, not in any one direction. It's important to have everything ready before you begin. I squeeze out new pigment to replenish my palette before I start because the paint needs to be juicy.

Take advantage of scraps of watercolor paper, used and unused, for this project. The paper should be thoroughly wet. I put mine under the faucet to saturate it. Sometimes I gently sponge away color on a used piece of paper and use the shadow colors as an underpainting.

Instead of painting to fit a cutout oval or rectangular format, create a pattern of random colors. When it's dry, lay the card on the art and move it around until just the right thing to fill the space emerges.

I find it much faster to compose letters on my computer. While a handwritten note is probably more acceptable, adding a "blob" or design to a plain piece of paper really brightens it up and makes it more personal. A whole piece of paper with drips and drops can be cut up and used for a myriad of purposes.

Prepare Your Paper

Saturate a quarter sheet of watercolor paper and lay it flat on your backing board. With a large brush or sponge gently brush out from the center going toward the edges to push away any bubbles underneath. It's important to wait a few minutes for the water to be absorbed before dropping the colors. The paper should have a dull sheen all over. Be patient, if the paper is too wet the color will run out too far.

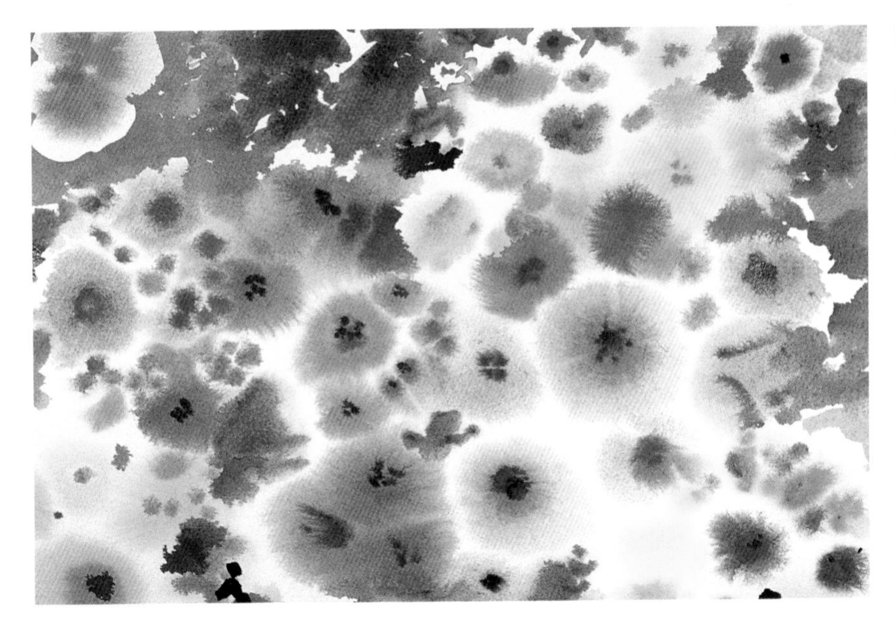

STEP ONE

Load your brush with pigment and either squeeze it out and let it drop onto the paper or gently touch the loaded brush to the paper. Begin around the edges because that's the first area to dry. The paint will burst outward and create flowerlike shapes. Several drops in the same area enlarge the shape. Also, other colors dropped on top of the original drips create centers or multicolored flowers.

The flower in the upper left is an example of three colors dropped near or on top of one another. The green surrounding the flower was added later.

The bright red flower in the upper right seems out of place, so I stopped using it.

STEP TWO

When the painting is dry, lay the cutout card over your work. The flower in the upper left seems just right for this dark blue card. Lightly pencil around and cut it out, leaving at least ¼" (6mm) border to paste inside the card.

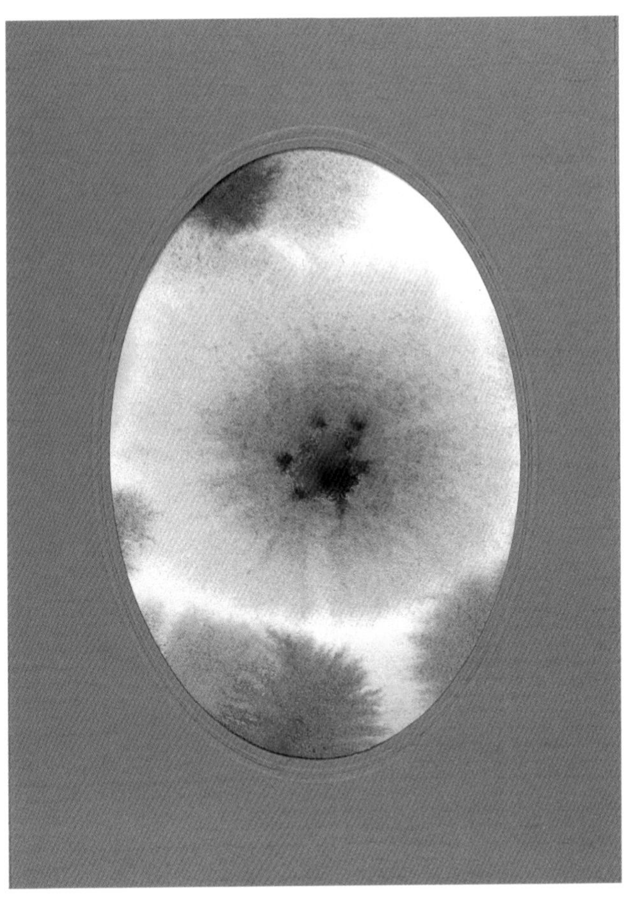

STEP THREE

Turn the artwork and move the oval cutout card around to find other possibilities.

When Drips Drop Ideas

Make Your Own Watercolor Paper Card

STEP ONE

Cut out an opening in a card made from 140-lb. (300g/m²) watercolor paper that can be folded into thirds.

STEP TWO

Pencil around the opening.

STEP THREE

Mask around the opening, one side at a time, and use a felt-tip marker or watercolor to create a simple design.

FINAL

Tape the painting inside the card. Use double-sided sticky tape or glue to seal the flap over the back of the painting.

I used at least thirteen more pieces from the same artwork to make note cards, invitations, gift cards, and even a picture for a key chain frame. I used a plastic drafting half-circle as a guide to cut out the semicircles. Here and on the next two pages are some examples to get your imagination going.

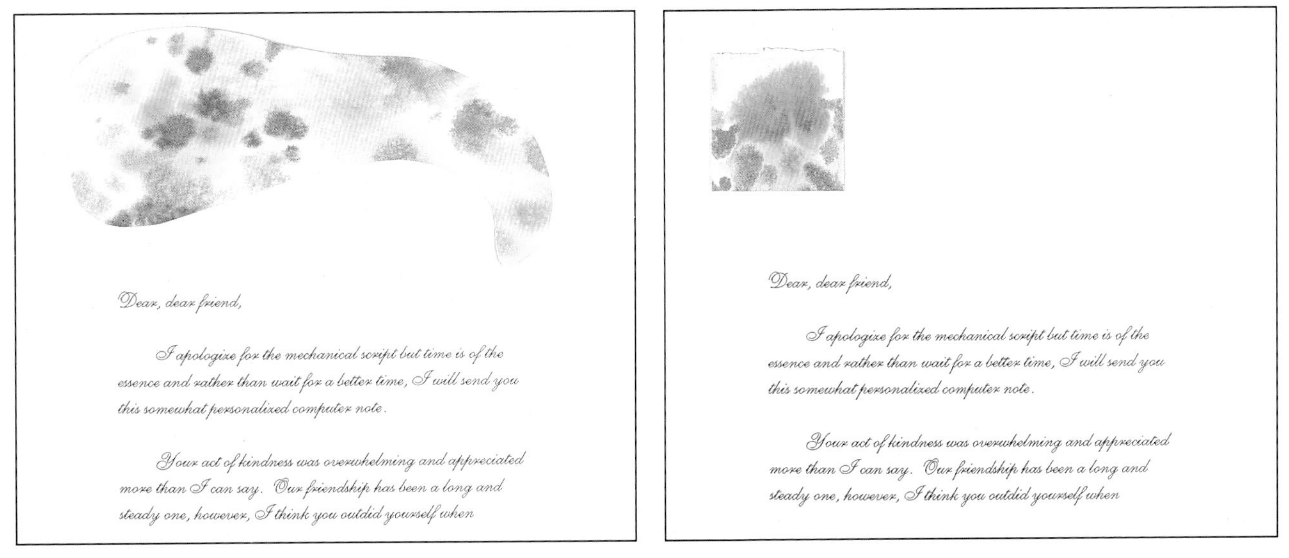

Dear, dear friend,

I apologize for the mechanical script but time is of the essence and rather than wait for a better time, I will send you this somewhat personalized computer note.

Your act of kindness was overwhelming and appreciated more than I can say. Our friendship has been a long and steady one, however, I think you outdid yourself when

Dear, dear friend,

I apologize for the mechanical script but time is of the essence and rather than wait for a better time, I will send you this somewhat personalized computer note.

Your act of kindness was overwhelming and appreciated more than I can say. Our friendship has been a long and steady one, however, I think you outdid yourself when

You can brighten up a computer written letter by cutting out an interesting shape and pasting it on the top of the letter.

Cut out a square and stick it in the upper-left corner of the letter.

Dear, dear friend,

I apologize for the mechanical script but time is of the essence and rather than wait for a better time, I will send you this somewhat personalized computer note.

Your act of kindness was overwhelming and appreciated more than I can say. Our friendship has been a long and steady one, however, I think you outdid yourself when

Cut out a larger square that resembles a flower and paste it in the middle.

More Ideas When Drips Drop

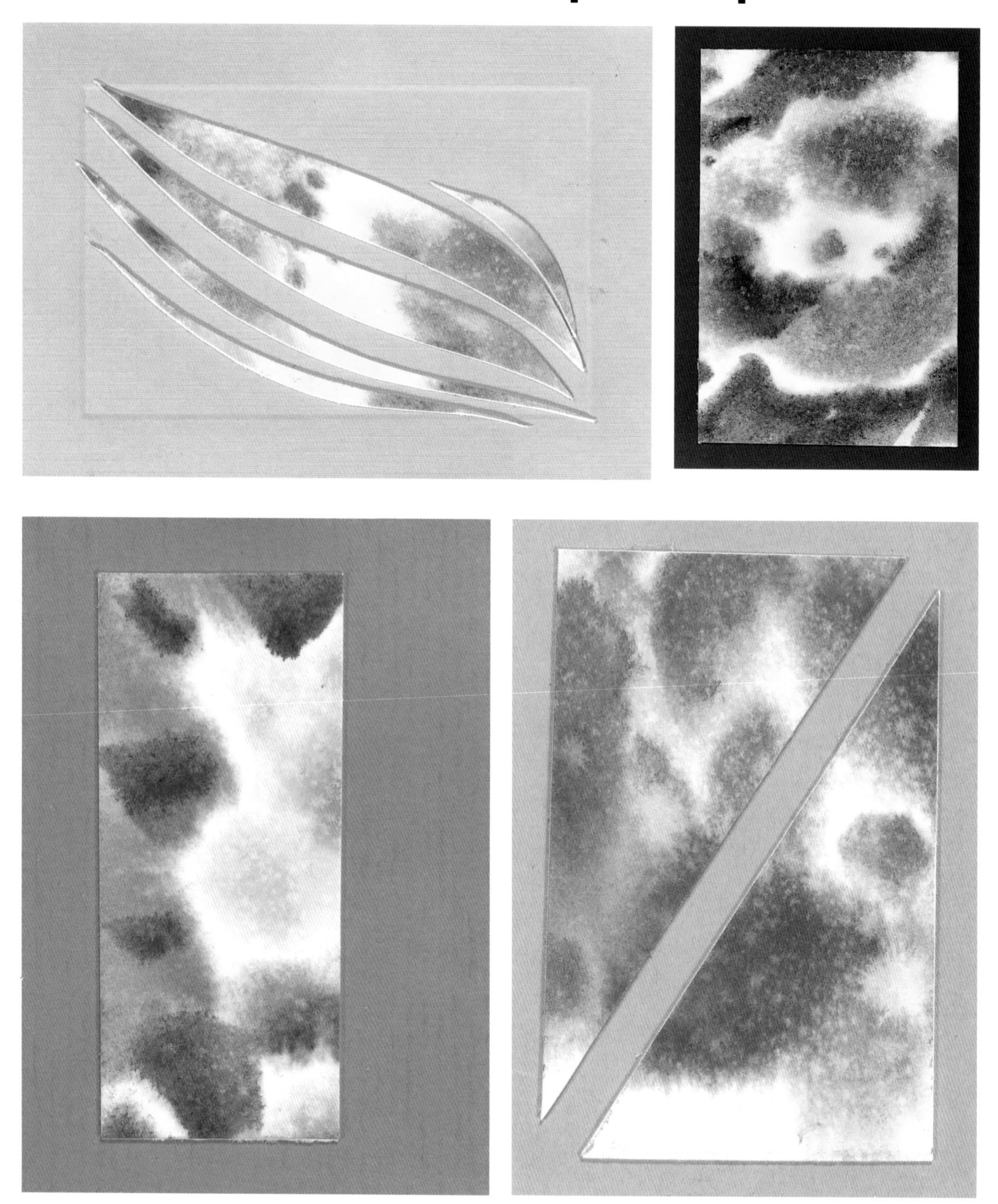

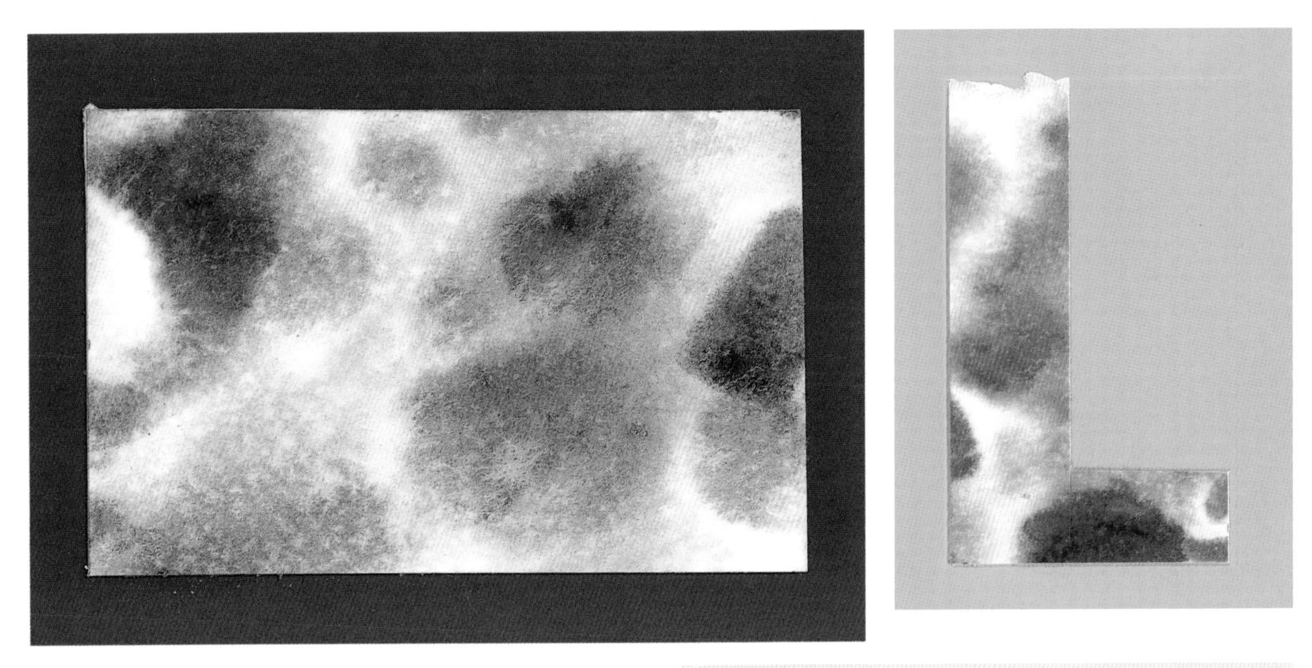

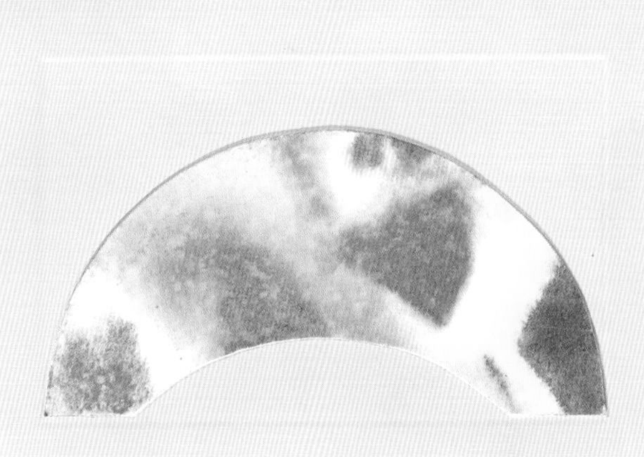

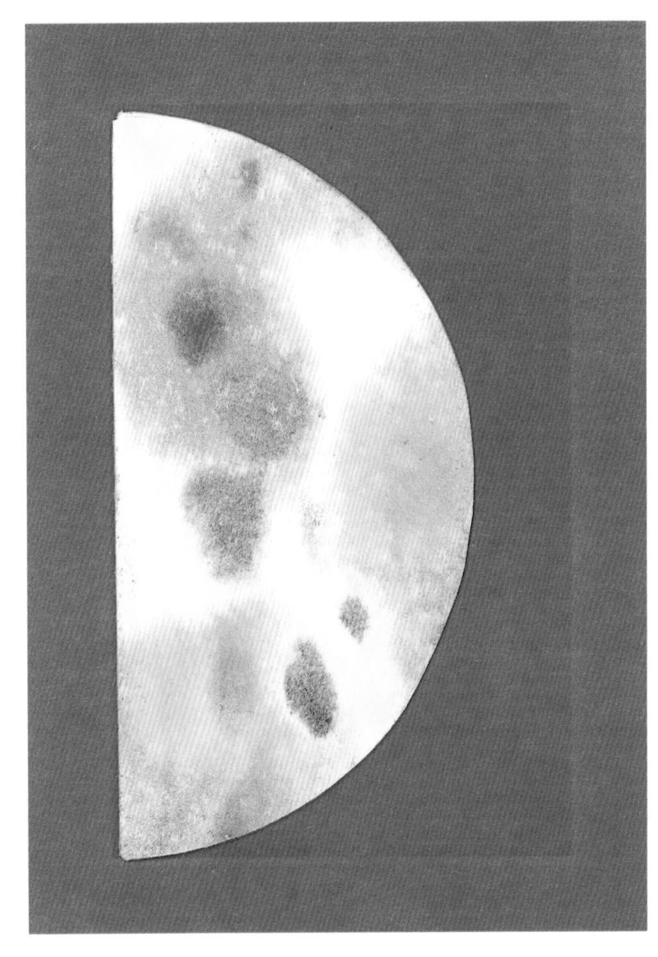

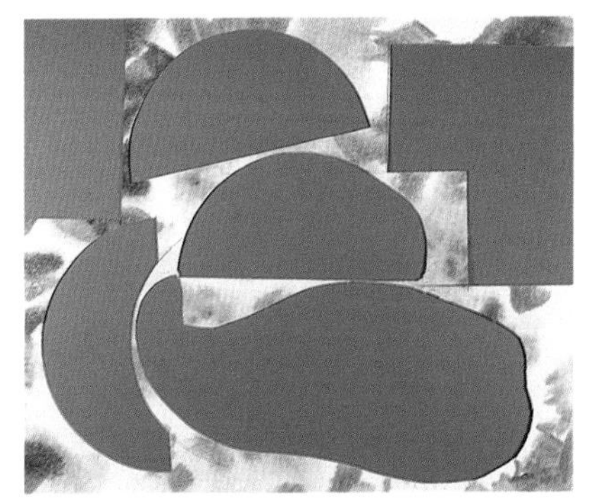

This is what is left of the When Drips and Drop artwork. Nothing is wasted.

PROJECT THIRTY-FOUR

Pure Fantasy

To make the following fantasy cards use random color brushed and dropped on wet or partially wet paper, allowing some white to show. A limited palette of gouache is used to paint the opaque figure over the watercolor.

The small figure is quite simple and easily mastered, so several can be made at a time. All the white areas on the painting can be painted first; then the pale blue; then the arms and legs and finally the ribbons, shoes and socks. To do several of these fantasy cards for a special birthday party would not take much time. A bird, butterfly or animal could be substituted for a little girl or boy.

This art can be turned into great little gifts, too, by using those inexpensive self-standing plastic frames. They come in several sizes. In this exercise I used 3¼" × 2¼" (8.3cm × 5.7cm) and 5" × 3½" (12.7cm × 8.9cm). Remove the photo that comes with the frame and place it on a clean piece of paper. Trace around the edges. Cut the center out, making a frame. Place this frame on the completed artwork as a reference to find interesting color compositions for the small figure.

STEP ONE

Tape one-eighth of a sheet of watercolor paper (7½" × 11" or 19.1cm × 27.9cm) to the backing board. Randomly wet areas of the paper with a brush or sponge, leaving areas of dry paper that will remain white. Drop and/or paint in colors such as mauve, Permanent Rose, Winsor Red and Winsor Green mixed with Raw Sienna and/or Ultramarine Blue. The paper will buckle, but if you allow it to dry or dry it with a hair dryer, it will flatten out again.

After the painting is dry, place the format cutout over the art and look for interesting color compositions to place a tiny figure on. Pencil around the areas.

ADD GOUACHE

I used a very limited palette of gouache to paint the opaque figure over the watercolor: Winsor & Newton's Permanent White, Jet Black, Ultramarine Blue, Lemon Yellow and Alizarin Rose Madder Red.

STEP TWO

Use white gouache and paint the hat and dress of the little girl. The hat is a small circle, the top of the bodice is a soft triangle that leans to the left under the hat, and the skirt is a lopsided bell shape.

STEP THREE

An oval of light blue is painted on the bottom of the skirt to show that the girl is bending over. Using the same color, paint a backwards *C* on the brim of the hat to create the crown as well as a little under the left bodice. The legs are simple straight lines and the arms are angled lines. The flesh color is made with a mixture of white, yellow, red and very little blue.

STEP FOUR

Add a blue ribbon on the hat and waist. Paint white dots for socks and black dash-like shapes for the shoes, and we have a small girl who stands on a petal, looking into the center of an imaginary flower, gesturing in wonderment and joy.

FINAL

Six little ladies take their places on this one sheet of fantasy flowers. There are three small paintings for the small frames, two paintings for the larger frames. In the middle is a bookmark that can be slipped into a book as a gift for a special child, and the last picture area becomes a personalized gift card. The paintings can also be mounted on greeting or note cards.

PROJECT THIRTY-FIVE

Pure Fantasy Another Way

STEP ONE

Trace the figure of a small boy. In this case, the drawing is too big and is reduced on a photocopy machine.

STEP TWO

Wet an eighth sheet of watercolor paper thoroughly. When the paper absorbs the water and loses its glossy sheen, paint a mixture of Ultramarine Blue and a little Burnt Sienna in circles, leaving the centers white.

STEP THREE

Working quickly, while the paper is still wet, drop in the centers using red first and then a mixture of mauve and Burnt Sienna. The flowers are further defined by adding different mixtures of green around them, allowing blue to remain around the edge of the petals.

STEP FOUR
Paint the little boy using gouache pigments. Start with the head and paint an oval shape of skin color. Leave a space for the white collar and paint the boy's suit with a mixture of blue and just a little white. Dry the paper, and then paint the legs, hand, white collar and dark brown hair. Dry it again, then paint blue socks and black shoes. To create the effect of plaid, paint tiny strokes up and across the suit using black, white and green. Paint the negative shape just above the boy's feet to create a place for him to stand on a leaf.

This shows the entire sheet of paper filled with an assortment of shapes for cards or gifts.

The completed card.

Pure Fantasy Ideas

A gift for you

JACQUELINE PENNEY

PROJECT THIRTY-SIX

Poetic Justice

A short poem, prayer or simple phrase can be made into a very special card or framed gift.

When I asked my painting partners to share some of their more meaningful journal inscriptions, they came up with several. Words trigger the imagination. Use very simple colored backgrounds to provide a setting for the words that emphasizes their message.

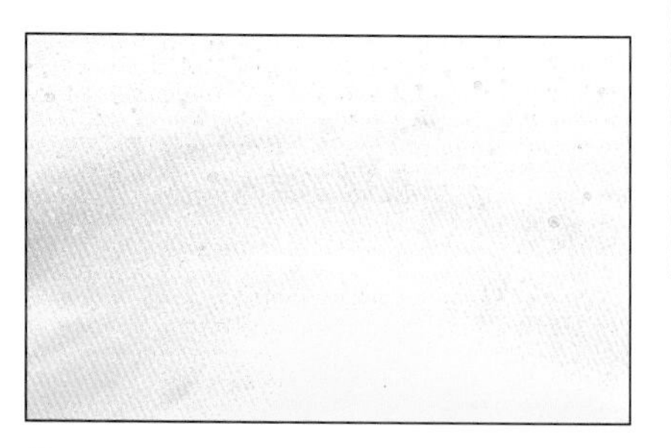

STEP ONE

To emphasize the words "Galaxy of stars," spatter masking fluid on the top of the card. Be sure to lay paper towels around the area to keep the spatter confined. When the paper is dry, paint pale pink and yellow curved brushstrokes. Dry.

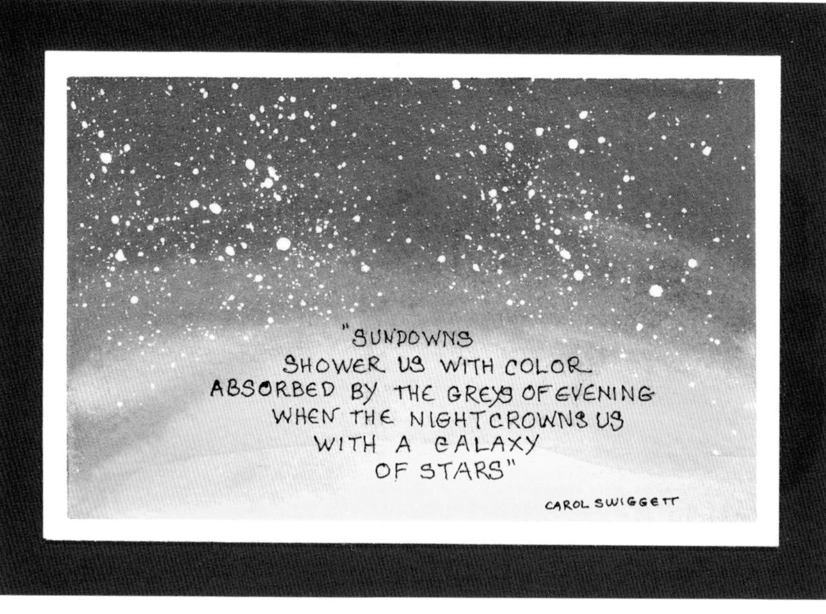

FINAL

Mix Ultramarine Blue and a little Permanent Rose and paint a graded wash starting at the top. While it's still wet, add a little brighter pink and yellow where needed. Dry the card thoroughly. Remove the masking fluid and lay a piece of tracing paper over your work. Print the quote in pencil to make sure the words line up nicely. Trace, if necessary, then print the quote in ink.

WORDS BY CAROL SWIGGETT. PAINTING BY JACQUELINE PENNEY.

This card by Henry Fukuhara uses words in a different way—as a fold-out letter. You could even use a fold out poem that corresponds to your painting.

PAINTING BY HENRY FUKUHARA

What could be simpler than "Thank You"? The underpainting is subtly dynamic with an angular thrust. The words are written with a no. 2 round. Thin lines are made with little pressure. Thick lines have more pressure applied on the down stroke.

"Our grief is the eternal testament that we have loved" can be artistically interpreted many ways. Just a few beautiful words can be very meaningful. A heart symbolizes love, and many variations on this theme are conceivable.

WORDS BY MARY O'SHAUGHNESSY. PAINTING BY JACQUELINE PENNEY

This beautiful card by Sylvia Geoghegan would be enjoyed by anyone. The sentiment "You cannot direct the wind. You can adjust your sails," is appropriate for many occasions.

CARD BY SYLVIA GEOGHEGAN

Painting mounted on colorful card with quote from Carl Jung fits into a plastic box frame.

PAINTED BY SISTER MAUREEN CAREY, O.P.

Love of painting is reason enough to paint anything, any size, any way, but eventually the paintings pile up and you'll need creative ways to use them.

Chapter Eight

IDEAS FOR PRESENTATION

How you present, display or offer a watercolor greeting card or gift will depend on why, when, where and to whom you give it.

Before beginning a project I think about the size and presentation. As we've demonstrated in this book, small watercolors can be beautifully presented in a variety of ways—from a simple piece of folded watercolor paper to a unique cube full of paintings.

MAT YOUR OWN

If you have a mat cutter and want to cut your own mats, you can save money *and* space. Buy one sheet of white or cream mat board and cut two pieces in the size you want. This will make a double mat. Mark the opening for the art on one piece, which will be the inside mat. Paint around the opening with an acrylic color mixture to complement the work you're framing. Let it dry and then cut it out. To finish, cut out the opening for the art on the second or outside mat 1/4" (6mm) larger than the opening on the inside mat.

Use acrylic paints for mat colors. From five pigments—yellow, red and blue, plus black to shade and white to tint—a myriad of color combinations can be mixed and matched to complement your work.

Use a complementary acrylic color mixture to paint the inside mat. Paint the front side on the lightly marked area to be cut, in this case 1½" (3.8cm) in from the edges. Dry the paint thoroughly with a hair dryer. A second coat is sometimes necessary.

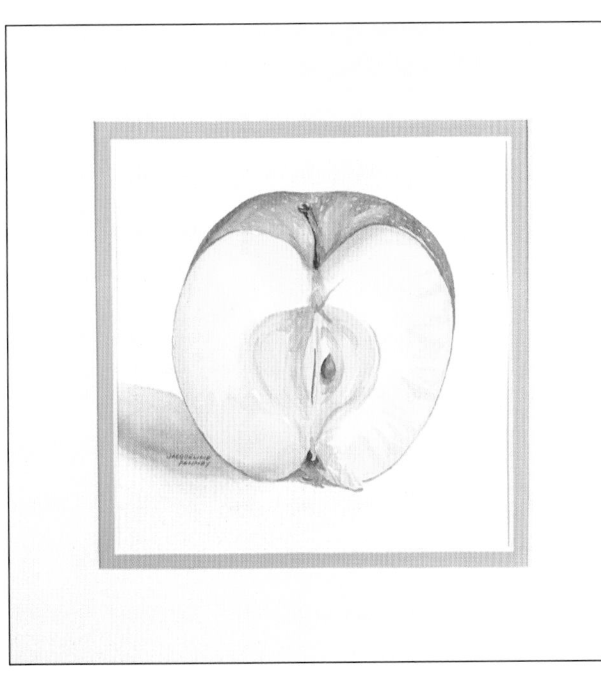

Cut the opening of the outside mat 1/4" (6mm) larger and you've made a double mat with custom color to go with the painting. It's inexpensive and looks great.

READY MADE MATS

Commercial precut presentation mats are available in many sizes and colors. The smallest mat can be made into two different size formats by punching out the small insert. You can wrap the matted paintings in plastic wrap and store them in a shoe box to pull out when you need them for a special gift.

The opening in this small mat with the insert in place is 1⅝" × 2⅝" (4.1cm × 6.7cm).

The insert can be popped out to make an opening of 2⅛" × 3⅛" (5.4cm × 7.9cm).

SHRINK WRAP TIP

Keep matted work clean and presentable by using kitchen plasic wrap. Place the matted artwork face down on the plastic at an angle. Fold the corners of the plastic wrap toward each other and heat with a hair dryer turned to hot. Use the dryer on the face of the work until all the wrinkles are stretched out.

Place matted artwork face down on the plastic at an angle. Fold the corners of the plastic wrap toward each other and heat with a hair dryer turned to hot.

Use the dryer on the face of the work until all the wrinkles are stretched out.

PROFESSIONAL FRAMING

Many times a special painting needs a special presentation. A professional framer will do wonders for a little gem. It will cost more, but you'll have a wide variety of frames from which to choose. Framers charge by the size of the artwork, so it will still cost less than having a large painting matted and framed. I recommend hanging one or two in your home to show prospective buyers what the little paintings will look like after framing.

One of my favorite quotes hangs on my kitchen wall: "I don't want to tiptoe through life only to arrive safely at death." I don't know who wrote this, but I like to be reminded that life is an adventure.

Conclusion

What Have You Got to Lose?

There are many reasons why I like to paint small works of art. A detailed, preliminary sketch or painting can be accomplished in a short amount of time and translated into a larger painting without losing motivation. As a bonus, I usually have two paintings to frame, one large and one small.

Formats for small paintings can be the same or vary considerably depending on the subject matter. I can apply several washes at a time. While one painting is drying, I can work on another with the same color combination or vary it completely. When I work this way, I find it stops me from overworking and keeps my focus fresh.

In her book *Drawing on the Right Side of the Brain*, Dr. Betty Edwards proved that drawing and painting are perceptual skills that can be taught. So, even if you think you don't have talent, you can learn to paint and draw. Small watercolors are a wonderful way to begin.

Two of my friends were at one time my students. Sylvia is a quadriplegic. She has limited use of her arms and hands but is in no way limited when it comes to painting. She does paint large pieces but admits her first love is for the "little ones."

Sister Maureen, a Dominican nun, is naturally gifted with good drawing and color skills and has a unique style of her own. She also studied calligraphy when she was young and by combining these talents she creates exceptionally beautiful cards, paintings and gifts of love. Due to her vow of poverty, however, she has few resources for art materials.

These two women are exceptionally motivated and are exceptional role models as well, inspiring us with their energy. In this book I've shared many reasons why painting small can be joyful and rewarding. Now it's your turn to create special cards and gifts. What have you got to lose?

Index